Student Activity ~~Gu~~ ~~CONS~~UMER SCIENCES OF DELAWARE

You

Living, Learning, and Caring

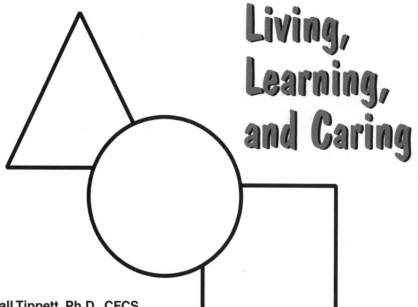

Deborah Tunstall Tippett, Ph.D., CFCS
Professor and Head
Department of Human Environmental Sciences
Meredith College
Raleigh, North Carolina

Martha Dunn-Strohecker, Ph.D., CFCS
Author of Family and Consumer Sciences Textbooks
and Management Consultant
Boston, Massachusetts

Publisher
The Goodheart-Willcox Company, Inc.
Tinley Park, Illinois

Introduction

This Student Activity Guide is designed for use with the text *You: Living, Learning, and Caring.* It will help you understand and remember the facts and concepts presented in the text. It will also help you apply what you have learned to your life now and in the future.

The activities in this guide are divided into lessons that correspond to the lessons in the text. By reading your assignment in the text first, you will have the information you need to complete the activities. Try to complete the activities without referring to the text. If you need to, you can look at the text later to complete any questions you could not answer. At that time, you can also compare your answers with the information in the text.

In this *Student Activity Guide,* you will find a variety of activities. Some activities will help you review text information. Other activities will let you apply what you have learned by making comparisons, evaluating, and expressing your opinions. Do your best to complete these activities accurately. Carefully follow the directions at the beginning of each activity.

The activities in this guide have been created to be both interesting and fun. They will let you express your creativity and develop skills related to a variety of topics. Some of the topics included in this guide are learning about yourself and children, being a responsible member of your family and community, and managing your resources. Other topics include information about the foods you eat, the clothes you wear, the place you live, and the job you may choose in the future. The more thought and effort you put into these activities, the more you will learn from them.

Contents

Topic 1 Learning About You

This Is Me

Activity A

Lesson 1-1

Name _____

Date _____ Period _____

Think about how you describe yourself and how others describe you. Then complete the following exercises and answer the question at the bottom of the page.

1. You have a pen pal in another country. Write a paragraph describing yourself that you will include in a letter to your pen pal. Describe your physical and personality traits. _____

   _____

   _____

   _____

   _____

   _____

   _____

2. You overhear one of your parents talking with a friend about you. How does your parent describe you?

   _____

   _____

   _____

   _____

   _____

   _____

3. Your best friend is describing you to a person you have not met. How does your friend describe you? List at least three traits your friend would use to describe you.

   a. _____

   b. _____

   c. _____

   How does the way you describe yourself differ from the way others describe you? Give reasons for these differences. _____

   _____

   _____

   _____

   _____

Personality Traits

Name _____

Date _____ Period _____

Read the list of personality descriptions below. If you believe the description is positive (good), put a *P* in the blank. If you believe the description is negative (bad), put an *N* in the blank. When this is done, complete the exercises at the bottom of the page.

_____ 1. is understanding of others

_____ 2. likes to brag

_____ 3. is a good listener

_____ 4. can play a joke on others, but cannot take a joke

_____ 5. likes to complain

_____ 6. compliments others

_____ 7. is friendly to everyone

_____ 8. smiles often

_____ 9. likes to gossip

_____ 10. is nosy

_____ 11. is a good winner and a good loser

_____ 12. is easy to talk to

_____ 13. tells secrets

_____ 14. talks only about himself or herself

_____ 15. is generous

_____ 16. is considerate of other people's feelings

_____ 17. is polite

_____ 18. is friendly one day and unfriendly the next

_____ 19. is a "know-it-all"

_____ 20. tells the truth

_____ 21. is bossy, must always be in charge

_____ 22. is reliable

_____ 23. keeps promises

_____ 24. looses temper often

_____ 25. is trustworthy

26. What is the number of one positive description you selected above? _____

 Explain why you think this describes a personality trait that is good to have. _____

 _____

27. What is the number of one negative description you selected above? _____

 Explain why you think this describes a personality trait that is not good to have. _____

 _____

 _____

 What could you do to change this negative trait? _____

 _____

 _____

A New Me

Name _____

Date _____ **Period** _____

Choose three physical traits and three personality traits you would like to improve. In the space below, write a plan to change each trait.

Physical Traits

1. I want to improve _____

    _____

    I plan to _____

    _____

    _____

2. I want to improve _____

    _____

    I plan to _____

    _____

    _____

3. I want to improve _____

    _____

    I plan to _____

    _____

    _____

Personality Traits

4. I want to improve _____

    _____

    I plan to _____

    _____

    _____

5. I want to improve _____

    _____

    I plan to _____

    _____

    _____

6. I want to improve _____

    _____

    I plan to _____

    _____

    _____

I Am an Adolescent

Name _____

Date _____ **Period** _____

Complete the following statements about how you are changing and growing.

1. I am an adolescent because _____
   _____
   _____

2. When I look in the mirror, I see someone who is _____
   _____
   _____

3. In the past year, I have made the following changes in my social growth: _____
   _____
   _____

4. In the past year, I have made the following changes in my intellectual growth: _____
   _____
   _____

5. In the upcoming year, I expect the following changes in my physical growth to occur: _____
   _____
   _____

6. The most important event in my life was _____
   _____
   _____

7. I feel like an adult when _____
   _____
   _____

8. I feel like a child when _____
   _____
   _____

9. What I dislike most about being an adolescent is _____
   _____
   _____

10. When I grow up, I want to be an adult who _____
    _____
    _____

Maturity Scale

Name _____

Date _____ Period _____

Answer the following questions about the way you believe you behave. Check either the *Yes, Sometimes,* or *No* column and add your points. Then answer the questions at the bottom of the page.

	Yes	Sometimes	No
1. Do I get along well with most adults?	_____	_____	_____
2. Do I stand up for my rights without being rude?	_____	_____	_____
3. Do I control my temper?	_____	_____	_____
4. Do I accept responsibility for my mistakes?	_____	_____	_____
5. Do I finish projects that I start?	_____	_____	_____
6. Do I obey rules at school?	_____	_____	_____
7. Do I obey rules at home?	_____	_____	_____
8. Do I get along well with my family?	_____	_____	_____
9. Do I solve most of my problems myself?	_____	_____	_____
10. Do I respect the opinions of others?	_____	_____	_____
11. Do I get along well with most of my friends?	_____	_____	_____
12. Do I keep promises to others?	_____	_____	_____
13. Do I practice being patient with others?	_____	_____	_____
14. Do I avoid complaining about my problems?	_____	_____	_____
15. Do I wait for what I really want?	_____	_____	_____
16. Do I apologize when I am wrong?	_____	_____	_____
17. Do I face my problems instead of making excuses?	_____	_____	_____
18. Do I feel self-confident?	_____	_____	_____
19. Do I try to adapt to different settings?	_____	_____	_____
20. Do I make friends easily?	_____	_____	_____
Total:	_____	_____	_____

For each *Yes* response checked, give yourself 5 points. For each *Sometimes* response checked, give yourself 3 points. For each *No* response checked, give yourself 0 points. The closer your score is to 100, the more mature you are.

What is the number of one of the questions to which you answered *No*? _____

How can you improve your behavior in this area? _____

_____

_____

How Do You Rate as a Family Member?

Name _____

Date _____ **Period** _____

Think about the contributions you make to your family. Then answer the following questions about yourself.

1. How do you share responsibilities in your family? _____
_____
_____

2. How do you show respect for the privacy of other family members? _____
_____
_____

3. In what ways do you respect and care for your possessions? _____
_____
_____

4. In what ways do you respect and care for family possessions? _____
_____
_____

5. Do you share thoughts and concerns with other family members? _____ If so, with whom do you
share these thoughts and concerns? _____
If you do share, how does this make you feel? _____
_____
_____

If you do not share, why not? _____
_____
_____

6. What consideration do you show in sharing the telephone with other family members? _____
_____

7. What consideration do you show in sharing the TV with other family members? _____
_____

8. How many hours have you spent with your family in the past month? _____

9. How many hours have you spent with your family in the past week? _____

10. What could you do to improve family relationships in your home? _____
_____
_____

Valuable Coupons

Name _____

Date _____ Period _____

Fill out the following coupons and give them to your parents. Choose ideas from the list below or make up your own.

- one breakfast in bed
- one week of dish washing
- one talk about the day's happenings at school
- three hours of free baby-sitting for a younger brother or sister
- the planning, preparation, and cleanup of one dinner
- one week free from arguments with brothers or sisters

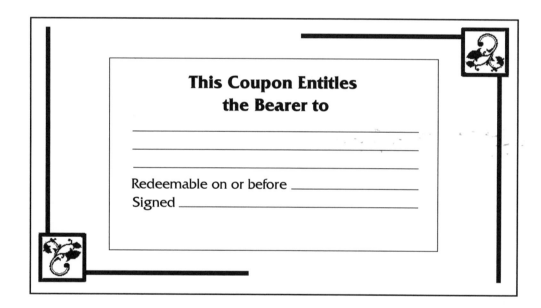

**This Coupon Entitles
the Bearer to**

_____
_____
_____

Redeemable on or before _____
Signed _____

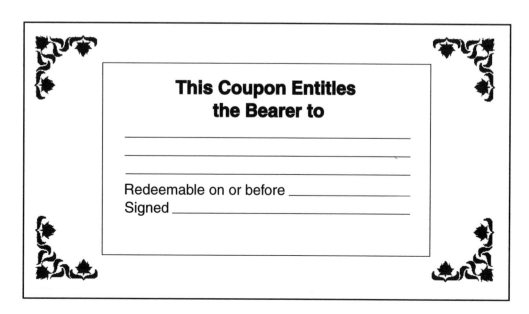

**This Coupon Entitles
the Bearer to**

_____
_____
_____

Redeemable on or before _____
Signed _____

Getting to Know Your Family

Activity C

Lesson 1-3

Name _____

Date _____ **Period** _____

To get to know the members of your family better, interview two family members. Ask them the following questions.

Family member A _____ Relationship _____

Family member B _____ Relationship _____

	Family Member A	**Family Member B**
1. What is your favorite color?	_____	_____
2. What is your favorite food?	_____	_____
3. What is your favorite magazine?	_____	_____
4. What is your favorite TV show?	_____	_____
5. What is your favorite sport?	_____	_____
6. What is your favorite hobby?	_____	_____
7. Who is your favorite musical performer?	_____	_____
8. What is your favorite book?	_____	_____
9. What is (was/will be) your favorite subject in school?	_____	_____
10. What is (was/will be) your favorite activity as a teen?	_____	_____
11. Who is (was/will be) your favorite teacher?	_____	_____
12. Who do you admire most?	_____	_____

Handling Family Problems

Activity A

Lesson 1-4

Name _____

Date _____ **Period** _____

You are ILTP (I Listen to Problems). Respond to the following letters by suggesting ways these adolescents might handle their family problems.

1. *Dear ILTP,*

    My parents are getting a divorce. I love them both. I'm afraid they will fight over who will get custody of me. I want to live with both of them. I don't want them to get divorced. Help!

    Signed,

    Afraid

    Dear Afraid,

    _____

    _____

    _____

    _____

    _____

2. *Dear ILTP,*

    My mother died three years ago. My dad is dating someone seriously. I don't want him to get married. I don't want a new mom.

    Signed,

    Motherless

    Dear Motherless,

    _____

    _____

    _____

    _____

    _____

3. *Dear ILTP,*

    My mother is an alcoholic. I'm embarrassed to have friends over. I hate her for doing this to me.

    Signed,

    Embarrassed

    Dear Embarrassed,

    _____

    _____

    _____

    _____

    _____

Solving Problems

Name _____

Date _____ Period _____

Sometimes families have problems. It is important to be able to solve these problems. Read each of the following situations and then answer the questions.

1. Mr. and Mrs. Irving have two children. Eileen is 12 and Rob is 15. For the past three years, Mr. Irving has had a drinking problem. Eileen and Rob are embarrassed to invite their friends to their house. Mrs. Irving pretends nothing is wrong.

   a. What is the family problem? _____

   _____

   b. How is each family member affected by it? _____

   _____

   c. What can be done to solve this problem? _____

   _____

   _____

2. Brendan Warring lives in a city apartment with his parents and his dog, Joey. Since the Warrings live in the city, Joey stays inside most of the time. It's Brendan's job to take care of Joey. Mrs. Warring has just found out she is allergic to Joey. Her doctor has advised the Warrings to give Joey away.

   a. What is the family problem? _____

   _____

   b. How is each family member affected by it? _____

   _____

   c. What can be done to solve this problem? _____

   _____

   _____

3. Vinnie is a single parent with a 13-year-old daughter named Allie. Vinnie has a good job as a manager of a local department store. Last week, he was notified that the store is going out of business and will be closing in two months.

   a. What is the family problem? _____

   _____

   b. How is each family member affected by it? _____

   _____

   c. What can be done to solve this problem? _____

   _____

   _____

Friendship

Think about what it means to be a good friend. Write sentences giving examples of what friends do for one another. Make the first letter of your sentences spell the word *friendship*. The first sentence is completed for you.

F riends help each other. _____

_____

R _____

_____

I _____

_____

E _____

_____

N _____

_____

D _____

_____

S _____

_____

H _____

_____

I _____

_____

P _____

_____

School Friends

Name _____

Date _____ Period _____

Write a brief description of each of the following school friends. Tell how each person's behavior helps or hurts his or her friendships with others.

Larry Late _____

_____

_____

_____

_____

Betty Borrower _____

_____

_____

_____

_____

Sam Selfish _____

_____

_____

_____

_____

Carl Cooperate _____

_____

_____

_____

_____

Ivan Interrupt _____

_____

_____

_____

_____

(Continued)

Sara Superior _____
_____
_____
_____
_____

Curt Courteous _____
_____
_____
_____
_____

Paul Prepared _____
_____
_____
_____
_____

Susan Spirit _____
_____
_____
_____
_____

Sammy Shy _____
_____
_____
_____
_____

Communicating Emotions

Name _____

Date _____ Period _____

You can communicate different emotions. From the list below, choose three emotions that can be communicated verbally and three emotions that can be communicated nonverbally. Describe how each emotion can be communicated.

love	security	nervousness	hate
hurt	jealousy	pessimism	anger
confusion	excitement	apathy	happiness
guilt	worry	optimism	hope
boredom	fear	depression	fulfillment

Emotions That Can Be Communicated Verbally

1. _____

2. _____

3. _____

How Emotions Can Be Communicated Verbally

1. _____
   _____
   _____
   _____

2. _____
   _____
   _____
   _____

3. _____
   _____
   _____
   _____

Emotions That Can Be Communicated Nonverbally

1. _____

2. _____

3. _____

How Emotions Can Be Communicated Nonverbally

1. _____
   _____
   _____
   _____

2. _____
   _____
   _____
   _____

3. _____
   _____
   _____
   _____

Communication Plus

Name _____

Date _____ Period _____

Read the following verbal and nonverbal responses. Put a plus sign (+) beside the responses you believe would contribute to good, healthy communication. Put a minus sign (–) beside the responses you believe would hinder or hurt communication. Then answer the questions at the bottom of the page.

_____ 1. smiles

_____ 2. makes hurtful remarks

_____ 3. raises eyebrows

_____ 4. nods

_____ 5. has a "no care" attitude

_____ 6. uses kind words

_____ 7. uses harsh words

_____ 8. frowns

_____ 9. laughs

_____ 10. is threatening

_____ 11. is helpful

_____ 12. is polite

_____ 13. interrupts

_____ 14. ignores the other person

_____ 15. acts bored

_____ 16. has a pleasant tone of voice

_____ 17. makes good eye contact

_____ 18. makes judgments

_____ 19. puts others down

_____ 20. asks questions to check understanding

21. What three types of behavior listed above would you like to see people use more often?

a. _____

b. _____

c. _____

22. How do these three types of behavior help communication?

a. _____

_____

b. _____

_____

c. _____

_____

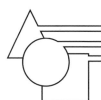

Topic 2 Learning About Children

A Cry for Help

Activity A

Lesson 2-1

Name _____

Date _____ **Period** _____

Unscramble the words to discover what causes babies to cry. Then give a hint for responding to the cry for help.

1. N Y H U G R _____

   Hint: _____

   _____

2. E T W _____

   Hint: _____

   _____

3. L D C O _____

   Hint: _____

   _____

4. I R F T G E N H D E _____

   Hint: _____

   _____

5. C E U M F R T O N A B O L _____

   Hint: _____

   _____

6. R E D O B _____

   Hint: _____

   _____

Bringing Up Baby

Name _____

Date _____ Period _____

Interview the parent of an infant. Ask the following questions and write the responses in the spaces provided.

Parent's Name _____

Infant's Name _____

1. How old is your baby? _____

2. What tasks has your baby learned in the past month? _____

   _____

   _____

   _____

   _____

3. What tasks has your baby learned in the past week? _____

   _____

   _____

   _____

   _____

4. How is your baby dependent on you? _____

   _____

   _____

   _____

   _____

5. What changes have you made in your life since the baby was born? _____

   _____

   _____

   _____

6. What changes has your family made since the baby was born? _____

   _____

   _____

   _____

   _____

Choices for Toddlers

Name _____

Date _____ Period _____

Think about how you would handle the following situations involving toddlers. Circle the letter of the best response and then explain why you chose it.

1. You are getting ready to take your two-year-old sister, Carrie Jo, to the park. It is cold outside and she needs a jacket. What is the best way to ask Carrie Jo to wear a jacket?

    a. "Do you want to wear a jacket?"

    b. "Which jacket do you want to wear, your red one or your blue one?"

    c. "If you don't wear a jacket, you'll get sick and have to go to the hospital."

    Why did you choose this answer? _____

    _____

    _____

2. You are feeding your two-year-old nephew, Tyler, a snack. What is the best question for you to ask him?

    a. "Which do you want, a graham cracker or a piece of candy?"

    b. "Do you want one cracker or two?"

    c. "What do you want to eat?"

    Why did you choose this answer? _____

    _____

    _____

3. You are baby-sitting Olga, who is three years old. It is almost time for her mother to return. You want to clean up. What can you say to get Olga to help you?

    a. "Let's pick up the toys together."

    b. "If you don't pick up the toys right now, the big bad wolf will get you!"

    c. "Shall we pick up the toys now or when your mother gets home?"

    Why did you choose this answer? _____

    _____

    _____

4. You are outside playing with your three-year-old neighbor, Marvin. He wants to ride his tricycle in the street. What should you say?

    a. "Don't ride in the street. You'll get run over."

    b. "If you ride your tricycle in the street, I'll call a policeman to put you in jail."

    c. "Ride your tricycle on the sidewalk next to me. The street is not a safe place to ride."

    Why did you choose this answer? _____

    _____

    _____

Discipline Secret

Name _____

Date _____ Period _____

Use the following code to decode the secret discipline message. After you have decoded the message, write two more hints for helping children achieve good behavior.

A	B	C	D	E	F	G	H	I	J	K	L	M
1	2	3	4	5	6	7	8	9	10	11	12	13

N	O	P	Q	R	S	T	U	V	W	X	Y	Z
14	15	16	17	18	19	20	21	22	23	24	25	26

23 8 5 14   25 15 21   3 15 18 18 5 3 20

1   3 8 9 12 4 19   2 5 8 1 22 9 15 18

25 15 21   13 21 19 20   6 15 12 12 15 23

20 8 18 15 21 7 8   23 9 20 8   23 8 1 20

25 15 21   19 1 25

1. _____

_____

2. _____

_____

_____

Observing Children

Name _____

Date _____ **Period** _____

Visit a preschool or child care center classroom. Observe the children and activities. Then answer the questions below.

1. What is the name of the preschool or child care center? _____
   _____

2. How old are the children you observed? _____
   _____

3. Describe the physical appearance of the children. _____
   _____
   _____

4. What activities did you observe? _____
   _____
   _____

5. How do you think these activities help children learn? _____
   _____
   _____

6. Talk to one of the children. Describe his or her vocabulary skills. _____
   _____
   _____

7. Describe how the children played with each other. Did they seem to get along with one another and share the toys? _____
   _____
   _____

8. Describe a situation you observed that you believe is typical for children this age. _____
   _____
   _____

9. If you were a teacher in this preschool or child care center, what would you do to help the children develop independence and self-confidence? _____
   _____
   _____

10. Based on this visit, how would you evaluate this preschool or child care center? Explain your answer.
    _____
    _____
    _____

Helping Children Learn

Name _____

Date _____ Period _____

Unscramble the underlined words to complete the sentences about helping children learn. Write the unscrambled words in the spaces provided in the puzzle. Identify the secret word. Then write a sentence explaining how the secret word helps children learn.

1. Infants learn by using their <u>NESSES</u>.
2. Children need love and <u>NATTEIONT</u> to learn.
3. Babies <u>RCY</u> when they want something.
4. Toddlers need to <u>LOXPREE</u> their environment.
5. Children need to feel and <u>COTHU</u> objects.
6. Children learn through <u>TRAPICEC</u>.
7. <u>TAGNILK</u> to children helps them learn to communicate.
8. Children need experiences in decision-<u>KANGIM</u>.
9. Playing helps children <u>RANLE</u>.
10. Children <u>MITTEAI</u> adults.
11. Children need to be given <u>HOSECCI</u>.
12. <u>TONNICUG</u> games help children learn about numbers.
13. Children need to learn to care for <u>SEMTEVHELS</u>.

1. ___ ___ ___ ___ ___ ___ ___
2. ___ ___ ___ ___ ___ ___ ___ ___ ___
3. ___ ___ ___
4. ___ ___ ___ ___ ___
5. ___ ___ ___ ___ ___
6. ___ ___ ___ ___ ___ ___ ___ ___
7. ___ ___ ___ ___ ___ ___ ___
8. ___ ___ ___ ___ ___ ___
9. ___ ___ ___ ___ ___
10. ___ ___ ___ ___ ___ ___
11. ___ ___ ___ ___ ___ ___ ___
12. ___ ___ ___ ___ ___ ___ ___ ___
13. ___ ___ ___ ___ ___ ___ ___ ___ ___ ___ ___ ___

14. What is the secret word? _____

15. How does the secret word help children learn? _____

_____

_____

Book Evaluation

Name _____

Date _____ **Period** _____

Choose a book for a preschooler. Evaluate it using the rating scale below. Then answer the questions at the bottom of the page.

Name of book _____

Author _____

Publisher _____

Copyright date _____

Age level _____

Price _____

	Poor	**Good**	**Excellent**
1. The subject is familiar to a preschooler.	_____	_____	_____
2. The book teaches about the world around a preschooler.	_____	_____	_____
3. The book teaches good behavior.	_____	_____	_____
4. The book is entertaining.	_____	_____	_____
5. The plot is easy for a preschooler to follow.	_____	_____	_____
6. The words are easy to understand.	_____	_____	_____
7. The illustrations are realistic.	_____	_____	_____
8. The illustrations help a preschooler understand the story.	_____	_____	_____

9. Summarize the story in this book. _____

_____

_____

_____

_____

10. Would you buy this book for a child? _____

11. Explain why or why not. _____

_____

_____

_____

_____

Give and Take

Name _____

Date _____ **Period** _____

For each set of arrows below, write the name of a person you love in the blank above the arrows. In the arrow on the left, list four ways you show love for that person. In the arrow on the right, list four ways that person shows love for you.

I love _____

List four ways you show love for this person.

1. _____
2. _____
3. _____
4. _____

List four ways this person shows love for you.

1. _____
2. _____
3. _____
4. _____

I love _____

List four ways you show love for this person.

1. _____
2. _____
3. _____
4. _____

List four ways this person shows love for you.

1. _____
2. _____
3. _____
4. _____

I love _____

List four ways you show love for this person.

1. _____
2. _____
3. _____
4. _____

List four ways this person shows love for you.

1. _____
2. _____
3. _____
4. _____

Helping Children Express Emotions

Name _____

Date _____ Period _____

Read the following case studies and answer the questions about how to help children express their emotions.

1. Two-year-old Lupe is trying to build a tower out of small blocks. She is able to put one block on top of another. When she tries to put a third block on top of the other two, however, the tower falls. After the tower has fallen three times, Lupe starts to scream and throw the blocks.

   a. What emotion is Lupe trying to express? _____

   b. What is causing Lupe to feel this emotion? _____

   _____

   c. What would you do to help Lupe express this emotion in a more appropriate way? _____

   _____

2. Four-year-old Daniel wants to help you prepare dinner. He opens the refrigerator and starts getting out every food item stored inside. You scold Daniel by saying, "Don't take all the food out of the refrigerator. You are making a mess." Daniel responds by saying that he hates you.

   a. What emotion is Daniel trying to express by helping you prepare dinner? _____

   b. What emotion is Daniel trying to express when he says he hates you? _____

   c. Does scolding Daniel help him learn to express his emotions in a positive way? Explain why or why not.

   _____

   d. Other than scolding, how might you respond to Daniel when he begins taking food out of the refrigerator? _____

   _____

   e. What would you do to help Daniel express his emotions in more appropriate ways? _____

   _____

   f. What task could you give Daniel that would allow him to help safely? _____

   _____

3. Five-year-old Gina does not want to play in the yard. Her neighbors have a large dog that barks whenever Gina goes outside.

   a. What emotion is keeping Gina from playing in the yard? _____

   b. How could you help Gina handle this emotion? _____

   _____

4. Your four-year-old brother comes into the room while you are doing your math homework. You are becoming frustrated because you are not getting the right solutions to any of the math problems.

   How can you express your emotions in a way that will set a positive example for your brother?

   _____

Playground Safety

Name _____

Date _____ Period _____

Study the playground pictured below and list five safety hazards. Than answer the questions at the bottom of the page.

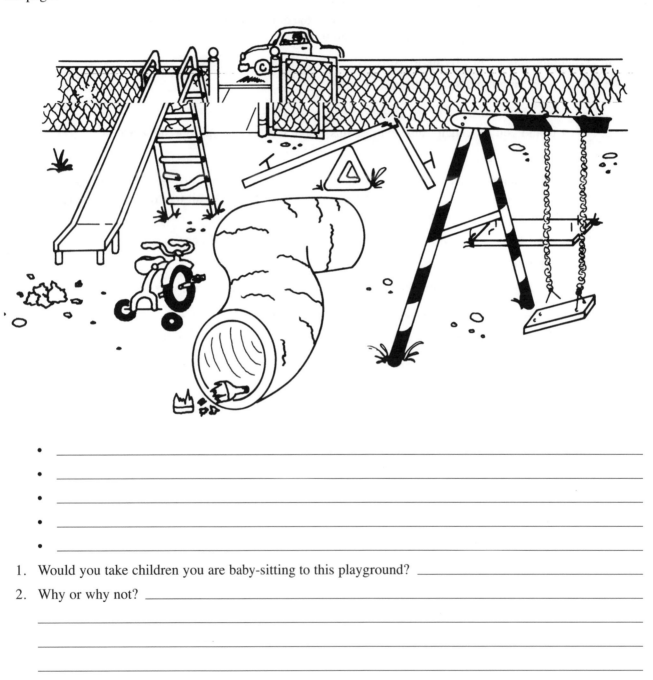

- _____
- _____
- _____
- _____
- _____

1. Would you take children you are baby-sitting to this playground? _____

2. Why or why not? _____

_____

_____

_____

Hire Me!

Name _____

Date _____ Period _____

Design a flyer advertising yourself as a baby-sitter. Be sure to include your experience and skills as a baby-sitter.

Hire Me
for Baby-Sitting

How Do You Rate as a Baby-Sitter?

Name _____

Date _____ Period _____

Answer the following questions about yourself and how you behave when you baby-sit. (If you've never been a baby-sitter, answer how you believe you would behave if you were a baby-sitter.) Check either the *Always, Almost Always, Sometimes, Almost Never,* or *Never* column and add up your points. Then answer the questions on the next page.

	Always	Almost Always	Sometimes	Almost Never	Never
1. Do you enjoy being with children?	___	___	___	___	___
2. Are you patient?	___	___	___	___	___
3. Do you understand how children grow and develop?	___	___	___	___	___
4. Do you act responsibly?	___	___	___	___	___
5. Do you show respect for others?	___	___	___	___	___
6. Do you handle emergencies well?	___	___	___	___	___
7. Do you visit the home of a family before you baby-sit for the first time?	___	___	___	___	___
8. Do you discuss your rate of pay before you baby-sit?	___	___	___	___	___
9. Do you find out about each child's eating and sleeping habits before you baby-sit?	___	___	___	___	___
10. Do you ask parents for emergency telephone numbers and a telephone number where they can be reached?	___	___	___	___	___
11. Do you eat only food that the parents have left for you?	___	___	___	___	___
12. Do you make only necessary telephone calls?	___	___	___	___	___
13. Do you handle breakable items carefully?	___	___	___	___	___
14. Do you stay with the children unless they are sleeping?	___	___	___	___	___
15. Do you play with the children?	___	___	___	___	___
16. Do you contact the child's parents immediately in a case of an accident or illness?	___	___	___	___	___
17. Do you follow safety rules?	___	___	___	___	___
18. Do you give children medicine only if the parents have instructed you to?	___	___	___	___	___
19. Do you praise the children whenever possible?	___	___	___	___	___
20. Do you cancel a job only if an emergency occurs?	___	___	___	___	___
Total:	___	___	___	___	___

(Continued)

For each *Always* checked, give yourself 4 points. For each *Almost Always* checked, give yourself 3 points. For each *Sometimes* checked, give yourself 2 points. For each *Almost Never* checked, give yourself 1 point. For each *Never* checked, give yourself 0 points.

If you scored

80, you are perfect, too good to be true.

70–79, you are an excellent baby-sitter. You will be in much demand.

60–69, you are a good baby-sitter.

35–59, you need improvement. Work on those items for which you scored a 2 or below.

34 or below, you need to work on those items for which you scored a 2 or below. When you have improved your score, baby-sitting might be a possible job for you.

21. List an item for which you scored a 2 or below. _____

_____

22. What could you do to improve in this area? _____

_____

_____

_____

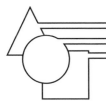

Topic 3 Making Decisions

Bag of Wants

Activity A

Name _____

Lesson 3-1

Date _____ **Period** _____

Make a list of items you would like to own in one month, one year, and five years. Then answer the questions at the bottom of the page.

I would like to own the following items within one month: _____

_____

_____

_____

_____

I would like to own the following items within one year: _____

_____

_____

_____

_____

I would like to own the following items within five years: _____

_____

_____

_____

_____

1. How do you plan to buy these items? _____

_____

_____

_____

2. How have your experiences affected your wants? _____

_____

_____

_____

3. What are three items you would like to have in the next five years that do not require money? _____

_____

_____

_____

Emotional Needs

Name _____

Date _____ Period _____

Think about how you can meet emotional needs. Below is a list of activities. Identify which emotional need(s) you can meet with each activity. Evaluate if the activity is a good or poor way to meet the emotional need(s). Then answer the questions at the bottom of the page.

Activity	Emotional Need(s)	Good or Poor Way
1. Joining a club		
2. Being student council president		
3. Bragging		
4. Reading an adventure novel		
5. Buying a bike lock		
6. Having a temper tantrum		

7. Write down one activity from above that is a good way to meet an emotional need. _____

_____

Explain your answer. _____

_____

_____

8. Write down one activity from above that is a poor way to meet an emotional need. _____

_____

Explain your answer. _____

_____

_____

Resources

Name _____

Date _____ Period _____

Below is a list of resources. Write each resource in the appropriate column of the chart to identify the type of resource it is. Then answer the questions at the bottom of the page.

artistic talent	courage	house	park
bicycle	creativity	judgment	personality
books	credit card	knowledge	police protection
car	enthusiasm	leadership skills	responsibility
city library	gasoline	mall	roads
clean air	good attitude	manners	school
clothes	health	money	time management skills
communication skills	honesty	musical talent	wisdom
computer skills	hospital		

Human Resources		Nonhuman Resources	
		Private Resources	*Public Resources*

1. Which of the human resource listed above do you have? _____

   _____

2. Choose one of these human resources and explain how you can use it to meet needs and fulfill wants.

   _____

3. Which of the nonhuman resource listed above do you have? _____

   _____

4. Choose one of these nonhuman resources and explain how you can use it to meet needs and fulfill wants.

   _____

Human Resources Checklist

Name _____

Date _____ Period _____

Read the list of human resources below. Place a check beside five human resources that best describe you. Then answer the questions at the bottom of the page.

_____	energy	_____	skills
_____	intelligence	_____	flexibility
_____	thoughtfulness	_____	strength
_____	politeness	_____	artistic ability
_____	neatness	_____	musical ability
_____	kindness	_____	tactfulness
_____	creativity	_____	understanding
_____	friendliness	_____	cheerfulness

1. What are two human resources you would like your friends to have? _____

_____

_____

_____

_____

_____

2. What are three human resources you would like to develop? _____

_____

_____

_____

_____

_____

3. Choose one resource you would like to develop and write a plan for developing it. _____

_____

_____

_____

_____

_____

_____

_____

_____

Values Auction

Name _____

Date _____ Period _____

Pretend you have $4,000 to spend at a values auction. In the blank next to each value, write down the amount you bid for the value. Then compare your bids with others in the class. The value goes to the highest bidder.

What am I bid for

_____ freedom

_____ a high school education

_____ a college education

_____ marriage

_____ family

_____ religious freedom

_____ money

_____ friends

_____ one good friend

_____ strong family ties

_____ happiness

_____ privacy

_____ a fancy bike

_____ service to others

_____ Total

Goal Archery

Name _____

Date _____ Period _____

Think about your long-term goals and how you plan to reach them. Then write one of your long-term goals on the bull's-eye. On the arrows, write the short-term goals necessary to reach your long-term goal.

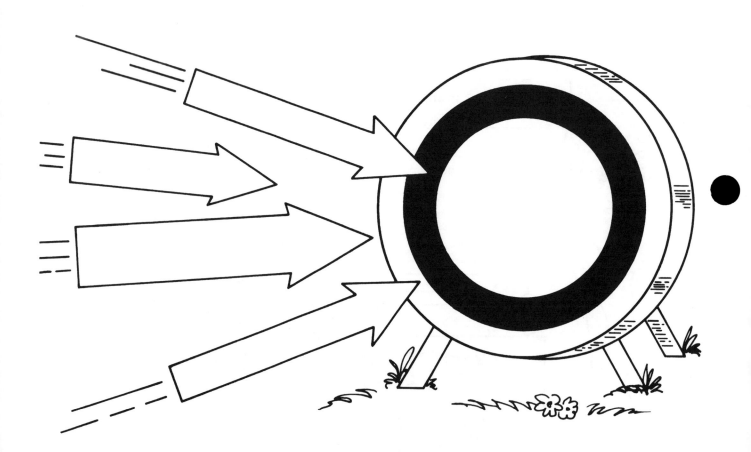

Decisions! Decisions!

Activity A

Name _____

Lesson 3-4

Date _____ **Period** _____

Complete the following statements about the decision-making process. Write the missing terms in the spaces provided in the puzzle. Identify the secret word. Then write a sentence explaining how the secret word relates to making decisions.

1. Make a decision based on your _____, needs, wants, values, goals, standards, and priorities.

2. A decision is a _____ made about what to do or say in a given situation.

3. You need to _____ all your alternatives.

4. Some decisions are made by _____.

5. When you give up one thing for another, you have a _____.

6. Make a list of _____ available to you.

7. There are six steps in the decision-making _____.

8. Consider advantages and _____ of your options.

9. Disadvantages are the _____ points.

10. _____ can help you learn how to make decisions.

11. _____ decisions you have made.

1. __ __ __ __ __ | __ | __ __ __
2. __ __ __ __ __ | __ |
3. __ __ | __ | __ __ __ __
4. __ __ __ __ | __ |
5. __ __ __ __ __ | __ |
6. __ __ __ __ __ | __ | __ __ __ __ __
7. __ __ __ __ __ | __ | __
8. __ | __ | __ __ __ __ __ __ __ __ __ __
9. | __ | __ __
10. __ __ __ | __ | __ __
11. | __ | __ __ __ __ __ __ __

12. What is the secret word? _____

13. How does the secret word relate to making decisions? _____

_____

_____

Make a Decision

Name _____

Date _____ Period _____

Think about the six steps of the decision-making process. Then read the case study about Raj and answer the questions at the bottom of the page.

Raj is in the eighth grade at Central Middle School. He earns above average grades in all his courses except math. His favorite after-school activity is playing baseball. He would like to play baseball in high school next year. However, school rules require athletes to pass all their classes to participate in a sport.

This summer Raj can take a special summer school course to help him with his math. He has also been given the chance to go to baseball camp. The camp takes place at the same time as summer school. Raj has one week before he has to sign up for either summer school or baseball camp.

1. What is Raj's problem? _____

2. What are two of Raj's alternatives?

   A. _____

   B. _____

3. List the advantages and disadvantages of each alternative.

   Alternative A
   Advantages: _____

   _____

   Disadvantages: _____

   _____

   Alternative B
   Advantages: _____

   _____

   Disadvantages: _____

   _____

4. If you were Raj, what would you decide? Why? _____

   _____

   _____

   _____

   _____

5. If Raj took your advice, what two steps would he still need to take to complete the decision-making process?

   _____

   _____

6. Why is it important to evaluate your decisions? _____

   _____

   _____

   _____

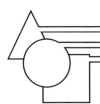

Topic 4 Managing Daily Living

Reaching a Goal

Activity A

Lesson 4-1

Name _____

Date _____ **Period** _____

Try using the management process to reach a short-term goal. First, select a goal, such as earning enough money to buy a new CD. Then follow the next steps of the management process. Write your plans below. After you have reached your goal, answer the last three questions.

1. What is your goal? _____

   _____

2. How do you plan to reach your goal? _____

   _____

   _____

   _____

   _____

3. What resources are you going to use to reach your goal? _____

   _____

   _____

   _____

4. How did you implement your plan? _____

   _____

   _____

   _____

   _____

5. How well did this plan help you in reaching your goal? _____

   _____

   _____

   _____

   _____

6. What would you do differently next time? _____

   _____

   _____

The "To Do" List

Name _____

Date _____ Period _____

Think about all the tasks you need to do tomorrow. List them below and check them off after you have completed them. Then answer the questions at the bottom of the page.

Completed	To Do

1. How did this list help you manage your time? _____

   _____

   _____

2. What else can you do to manage your time better? _____

   _____

   _____

Handling Stress

Name _____

Date _____ **Period** _____

You are ILTP (I Listen to Problems). Respond to the following letters by suggesting ways these teens might manage the stress in their lives.

1. *Dear ILTP,*

   I am so busy I don't know what to do. I have a different activity after school every day. I am an officer in some of the groups and have a lot of responsibilities. I never seem to have any time for myself.

   > *Signed,*
   >
   > *Too Busy*

   Dear Busy,

   _____

   _____

   _____

   _____

   _____

2. *Dear ILTP,*

   My family just moved to a new town. I don't know anybody. School starts next week. I'm really nervous about meeting new people.

   > *Signed,*
   >
   > *New Kid in Town*

   Dear Kid,

   _____

   _____

   _____

   _____

   _____

3. *Dear ILTP,*

   My grandmother just died. She lived with my family. We were very close, and I miss her a lot.

   > *Signed,*
   >
   > *Sad*

   Dear Sad,

   _____

   _____

   _____

   _____

   _____

Posture Checklist

Name _____

Date _____ Period _____

Choose a partner and rate his or her posture. Check either the *Yes* or *No* column and add up the points. Then answer the questions at the bottom of the page.

Did he/she	Yes	No
1. stand with chin up?	_____	_____
2. stand up straight with head held high?	_____	_____
3. stand with legs, shoulders, and back straight?	_____	_____
4. walk with head up?	_____	_____
5. walk with back straight?	_____	_____
6. walk with feet pointed straight ahead?	_____	_____
7. walk with arms swinging freely at side?	_____	_____
8. walk without shuffling or bouncing?	_____	_____
9. go up and down stairs with back straight?	_____	_____
10. use leg muscles to go up and down stairs?	_____	_____
11. use the handrail as a guide?	_____	_____
12. keep head up while going up and down stairs?	_____	_____
13. sit up straight?	_____	_____
14. sit down using leg muscles to support the body?	_____	_____
15. avoid slipping down in the chair while sitting?	_____	_____

For each *Yes* response checked, give your partner 1 point. For each *No* response checked, give your partner 0 points. The closer your partner's score is to 15, the better his or her posture is.

16. How can your partner improve his or her posture? _____

_____

_____

17. What can you do to help your partner improve his or her posture? _____

_____

_____

Grooming Skills

Name _____

Date _____ Period _____

Read the following statements about grooming. If the statement is true, place a *T* in the blank. If the statement is false, place an *F* in the blank. Then correct each false statement in the space below the statement.

_____ 1. Shave in the direction your hair grows.

_____

_____

_____ 2. Use a razor that is comfortable to hold and easy to use.

_____

_____

_____ 3. To prevent the razor from cutting or irritating your skin, apply shaving cream or a rich lather of soap.

_____

_____

_____ 4. There are special makeups for different skin types and problems.

_____

_____

_____ 5. Read the labels on makeup packages to make sure you have the right type for your skin.

_____

_____

_____ 6. To keep skin looking good, leave makeup on overnight.

_____

_____

_____ 7. To find the right makeup for you, it's a good idea to try your friend's first.

_____

_____

_____ 8. Dandruff and scalp diseases are often transferred by using other people's combs or brushes.

_____

_____

Looking Better All the Time

Name _____

Date _____ **Period** _____

Think about your appearance and how you would like to improve it. Then complete the exercise below.

I would like to improve (check all that apply)

_____ the condition of my skin

_____ my hairstyle

_____ the condition of my hair

_____ the condition of my teeth and gums

_____ the condition of my hands and feet

Choose two aspects of your appearance that you checked above. Then write a plan to improve each aspect.

1. I would like to improve _____

_____

I plan to _____

_____

_____

_____

2. I would like to improve _____

_____

I plan to _____

_____

_____

_____

Comparing Prices

Name _____

Date _____ Period _____

Compute the unit prices for each set of items below. Round prices to the nearest cent. (See page 126 of the text.) Then compare the unit prices to see which product is the better buy.

1. Shampoo

    a. Brand: New You

    Weight: 6 ounces

    Cost: $2.05

    Unit price: _____

    b. Brand: Smells So Good

    Weight: 12 ounces

    Cost: $3.35

    Unit price: _____

    The better buy is: _____

2. Deodorant

    a. Brand: Mighty Man

    Weight: 1.5 ounces

    Cost: $1.65

    Unit price: _____

    b. Brand: Fresh!

    Weight: 2.3 ounces

    Cost: $2.80

    Unit price: _____

    The better buy is: _____

3. Cereal

    a. Brand: Space Cadets

    Weight: 15 ounces

    Cost: $2.60

    Unit price: _____

    b. Brand: Nutty 'N Nutritious

    Weight: 25 ounces

    Cost: $3.25

    Unit price: _____

    The better buy is: _____

4. Chocolate Chips

    a. Brand: Chewy Chocolate

    Weight: 12 ounces

    Cost: $2.39

    Unit price: _____

    b. Brand: All Natural

    Weight: 6 ounces

    Cost: $1.50

    Unit price: _____

    The better buy is: _____

Researching a Product

Name _____

Date _____ **Period** _____

Read an article in a consumer magazine about a product. Then complete the following information and answer the questions at the bottom of the page.

Name of article _____

Date of article _____

Type of product tested _____

1. Write a brief summary of the article. Include a description of the tests performed on the product and the major findings. _____

   _____

   _____

   _____

   _____

   _____

   _____

   _____

   _____

   _____

   _____

   _____

   _____

   _____

   _____

   _____

   _____

   _____

2. Which brand of the product would you buy? _____

3. Why would you buy this brand? _____

   _____

   _____

   _____

Why I Buy

Name _____

Date _____ Period _____

Listed below are a number of items you may have bought recently. Select two of these items. Then explain how each of the following outside pressures might have affected your decision to buy these products.

toothpaste
chewing gum
greeting card
clothes
shoes

deodorant
soft drink
pens
snacks
board game

sports equipment
shampoo
TV
compact disc
magazine

1. Item: _____

   Peer pressure: _____

   _____

   _____

   Mass media: _____

   _____

   _____

   Advertising: _____

   _____

   _____

2. Item: _____

   Peer pressure: _____

   _____

   _____

   Mass media: _____

   _____

   _____

   Advertising: _____

   _____

   _____

Rights with Responsibilities

Name _____

Date _____ Period _____

Complete the chart below by explaining what each consumer right listed in the left-hand column means to you. Then in the right-hand column, list the responsibilities that go with each right.

Consumer Rights	Consumer Responsibilities
The Right to Choose	
The Right to Be Heard	
The Right to Safety	
The Right to Be Informed	
The Right to Redress	
The Right to Consumer Education	

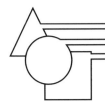

Topic 5 Managing Your Living Space

A House Is Not a Home

Activity A

Lesson 5-1

Name _____

Date _____ **Period** _____

List the differences between a house and a home in the blanks below. Cut out words and pictures from magazines that represent a house and words and pictures that represent a home. Use these words and pictures to make collages on the drawings below.

- _____
- _____
- _____
- _____
- _____

A house is. . .

A home is. . .

My First Apartment

Activity B

Lesson 5-1

Name _____

Date _____ Period _____

You have just rented your first apartment. Study the scale floor plan of this apartment below. Then answer the questions on the following page.

Scale: ¼″ = 1′0″

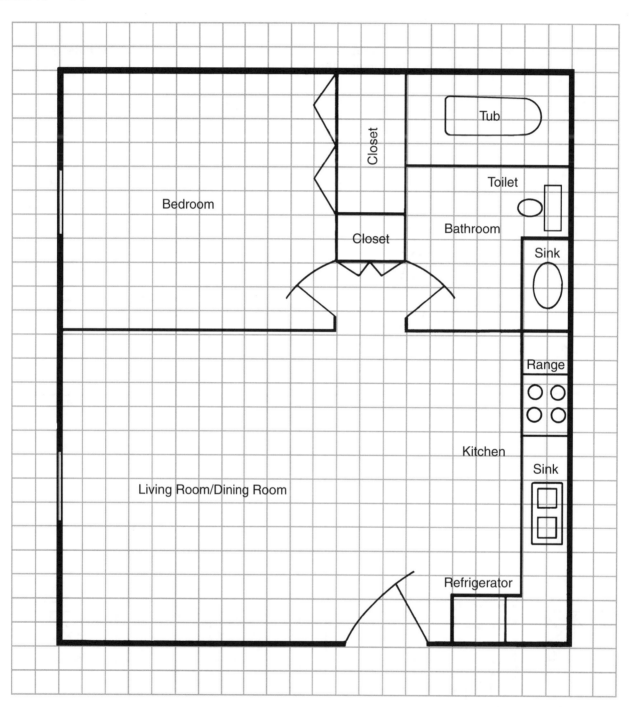

(Continued)

1. How many rooms are in your apartment? _____

2. List the rooms in your apartment. _____
   _____
   _____
   _____
   _____

3. List the private space(s) in your apartment. _____
   _____

4. List the shared space(s) in your apartment. _____
   _____

5. How many windows are in your apartment? _____

6. How many doors are in your apartment? _____

7. How many closets are in your apartment? _____

8. Where will you store the following items? _____
   a. Clothes _____
   b. Grooming supplies _____
   c. Food _____
   d. Dishes _____
   e. Towels and bedding _____
   f. Mop and broom _____

9. Do you think this apartment will meet your physical and emotional needs? Explain your answer. _____
   _____
   _____
   _____

Arranging Furniture

Name _____

Date _____ Period _____

You need to arrange your furniture in the apartment you just rented. Trace the pieces of furniture you want in your apartment from the group below. Cut out the pieces and color them. Then arrange the furniture on the scale floor plan on the next page. As you are arranging the furniture, keep traffic patterns in mind. Also consider the space needed for sleeping, dressing, eating, entertaining, and relaxing. When you have found a pleasing arrangement, glue the furniture pieces to the scale floor plan.

Scale: ¼″ = 1′0″

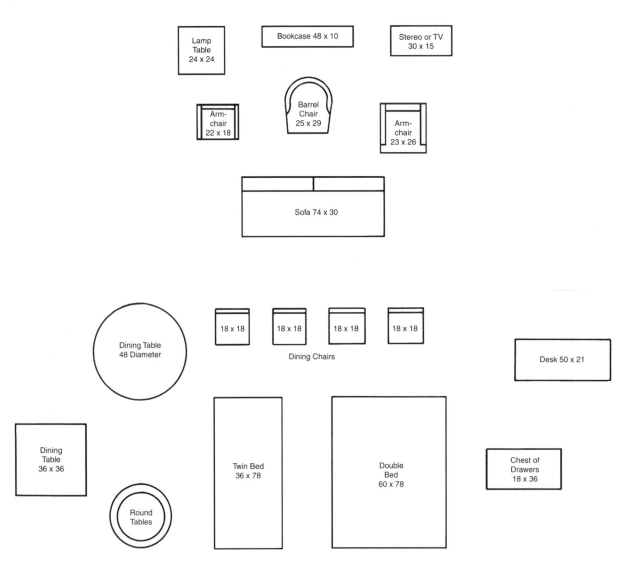

Copyright Goodheart-Willcox Co., Inc.

(Continued)

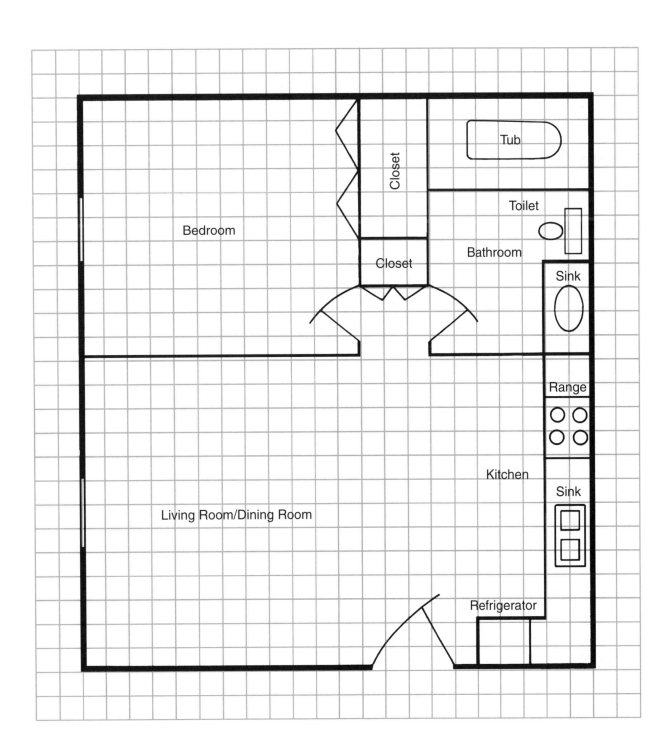

When Accidents Happen

Name _____

Date _____ **Period** _____

A guest speaker will be talking to your class about treating someone who has been injured in a household accident. Before the speaker arrives, review the questions below. Then at the bottom of the page, write two additional questions you would like to ask the speaker. As you listen to the speaker, write down the answers he or she gives to each question.

1. What first aid treatment should be given to someone who has fallen? _____

    _____

    _____

2. What should you avoid doing when someone has fallen? _____

    _____

    _____

3. What first aid treatment should be given to someone who has been burned? _____

    _____

    _____

4. What should you avoid doing when someone has been burned? _____

    _____

    _____

5. What first aid treatment should be given to someone who has been poisoned? _____

    _____

    _____

6. What should you avoid doing when someone has been poisoned? _____

    _____

    _____

7. What first aid treatment should be given to someone who has received an electric shock? _____

    _____

    _____

8. What should you avoid doing when someone has received an electric shock? _____

    _____

    _____

Write two additional questions you would like to ask the speaker.

a. _____

    _____

b. _____

    _____

Safety Checklist

Name _____

Date _____ Period _____

Evaluate your family's safety habits by answering each of the following questions. Check either the *Yes* or *No* column. Then answer the questions on the next page.

Do members of my family	Yes	No
1. secure loose rugs?	_____	_____
2. keep the stairs well lit?	_____	_____
3. use sturdy ladders and step stools?	_____	_____
4. clean up spills right away?	_____	_____
5. put safety gates at the top of stairs if there are young children at home?	_____	_____
6. have nonskid mats and/or decals in showers and bathtubs?	_____	_____
7. avoid running up and down stairs?	_____	_____
8. have smoke detectors installed?	_____	_____
9. have fire escape plans for day and night?	_____	_____
10. know the emergency telephone numbers?	_____	_____
11. avoid having too many plugs in one outlet?	_____	_____
12. avoid smoking in bed?	_____	_____
13. wait until ashes are cool to empty ashtrays?	_____	_____
14. follow instructions when using space heaters?	_____	_____
15. store toxic substances away from young children?	_____	_____
16. have safety latches on cabinets and drawers if there are young children at home?	_____	_____
17. avoid storing toxic substances in food containers?	_____	_____
18. avoid touching electric appliances with wet hands?	_____	_____
19. place covers on electric outlets if there are young children at home?	_____	_____
20. buy electric appliances with the UL label?	_____	_____
21. avoid using frayed electric cords?	_____	_____
22. keep all windows and doors locked?	_____	_____
23. leave a light on when the family is away at night?	_____	_____
24. avoid identifying themselves to strangers who call?	_____	_____
25. ask "Who is it?" before opening the door?	_____	_____
26. make sure that mail and newspapers are collected when on vacation?	_____	_____
27. share in the responsibility for keeping the home safe?	_____	_____

(Continued)

Choose three questions to which you responded *No*. Write plans to help your family improve in these areas.

28. Question # _____ : _____

_____

_____

_____

_____

29. Question # _____ : _____

_____

_____

_____

_____

30. Question # _____ : _____

_____

_____

_____

_____

Home Clean Home

Name _____

Date _____ **Period** _____

Think about how clean your home is. Then complete the following sentences about taking care of your home.

1. When my home is clean, I feel _____

   because _____

   _____

2. My bedroom is often _____

   _____

   _____

3. The person who does most of the cleaning in my home is _____

   because _____

   _____

4. I am a homemaker when I _____

   _____

   _____

5. At home, I am responsible for cleaning _____

   _____

   _____

6. The cleaning task I like least is _____

   because _____

   _____

7. The cleaning task I like most is _____

   because _____

   _____

8. I share cleaning tasks with _____

   _____

   _____

Just Do It!

Name _____

Date _____ Period _____

Read the case study about the Russos and make a cleaning schedule for them. List the daily and weekly tasks that need to be performed and decide which family member should do each task. Be sure to tell if the tasks will rotate.

Rosie and Ron Russo have two children, 10-year-old Christina and 4-year-old Jessica. They live in a three-bedroom, two-bathroom house. Rosie and Ron own and manage a restaurant. The restaurant is open from 7:00 a.m. to 9:00 p.m. Tuesday through Saturday and from noon to 8:00 p.m. on Sunday. It is closed on Monday.

Rosie and Ron have arranged their schedules so they can care for Jessica and Christina and work at the restaurant. Tuesday through Saturday, Ron leaves for work at 6:00 a.m. and returns home at 11:00 a.m. Rosie works from 11:00 a.m. to 4:30 p.m. Then Ron goes back to the restaurant until 10:00 p.m. On Sunday, Rosie works from 11:00 a.m. to 4:00 p.m. and Ron works from 4:00 p.m. to 9:00 p.m. They also do some of the bookkeeping for the restaurant at home. Christina attends school from 8:00 a.m. until 3:00 p.m. on weekdays.

Cleaning Schedule

Task	Monday	Tuesday	Wednesday	Thursday	Friday	Saturday	Sunday
Daily:							
Weekly:							

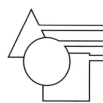

Topic 6 Living for Tomorrow

Effects of Pollution

Activity A

Lesson 6-1

Name _____

Date _____ Period _____

The chart below lists sources of pollution. Using the text and other sources, list the types of pollutants or waste materials each source might create. Then explain the effects these pollutants have on people.

Sources of Pollution	Types of Pollutants/Waste Materials	Effects On People
Homes		
Industry (factories and mills)		
Retail businesses (stores, hotels, and restaurants)		
Schools		
Transportation (cars, buses, airplanes, trains, and trucks)		
Recreation areas (beaches, campsites, and swimming pools		

Reducing Trash

Name _____

Date _____ Period _____

Give a suggestion for a reusable item you could use instead of each of the disposable items pictured below.

1. foam cup

    reusable item _____

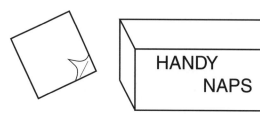

4. paper napkins

    reusable item _____

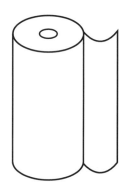

2. paper towels

    reusable item _____

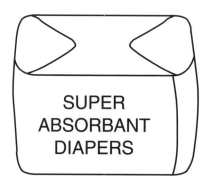

5. disposable diapers

    reusable item _____

3. paper or plastic shopping bag

    reusable item _____

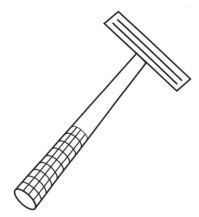

6. disposable razor

    reusable item _____

How Do You Care for the Environment?

Name _____

Date _____ Period _____

Answer the following questions about the ways you care for the environment. Check either the *Often, Sometimes,* or *Never* column. Then answer the questions at the bottom of the page.

	Often	**Sometimes**	**Never**
1. How often do you reuse products by			
a. carrying a reusable tote bag to the store when shopping?	_____	_____	_____
b. reusing wrapping paper, plastic bags, and/or boxes?	_____	_____	_____
c. giving old clothes to others?	_____	_____	_____
d. using the back sides of paper for notes?	_____	_____	_____
e. cutting up old sheets, towels, and/or clothes for dust cloths or cleaning rags?	_____	_____	_____
f. donating old books and magazines to hospitals, child care centers, and/or libraries?	_____	_____	_____
g. making art projects?	_____	_____	_____
2. How often do you reduce waste by			
a. buying products with less packaging?	_____	_____	_____
b. avoiding the purchase of hazardous chemical products?	_____	_____	_____
c. avoiding the purchase of disposable products, such as disposable razors and paper towels?	_____	_____	_____
d. buying refills?	_____	_____	_____
e. recycling products instead of throwing them away?	_____	_____	_____
3. How often do you take part in recycling efforts by			
a. separating recyclables from your regular trash?	_____	_____	_____
b. buying products made from recycled materials?	_____	_____	_____
c. buying from companies that demonstrate concern for the environment?	_____	_____	_____
d. writing companies about their lack of concern for the environment?	_____	_____	_____

4. What is another way you could reuse products? _____

_____

5. What is another way you could reduce waste? _____

_____

6. What is another way you could recycle products? _____

_____

Off, Please

Name _____

Date _____ **Period** _____

Design a small sign to go around the light switches in your home. This sign is to remind you to turn off lights when you are not in the room.

Energy Conservation Checklist

Name _____

Date _____ **Period** _____

Are you doing your part to conserve energy? Check your family's conservation habits by answering the following questions. Check either the *Yes* or *No* column. Then answer the questions on the next page.

Do you   **Yes**   **No**

1. turn off lights when not in the room?   _____   _____

2. turn off appliances when not using them?   _____   _____

3. walk or ride a bike instead of riding in a car whenever
    possible?   _____   _____

4. avoid changing the thermostat setting often?   _____   _____

5. have weather stripping around windows and doors?   _____   _____

6. keep drapes and shades closed at night in the winter?   _____   _____

7. keep furniture and window coverings from blocking
    heating vents?   _____   _____

8. turn the water heater off when away from home for
    several days?   _____   _____

9. keep drapes and shades closed during the day in the
    summer?   _____   _____

10. use fans instead of air conditioners whenever possible?   _____   _____

11. use hot water only when necessary?   _____   _____

12. when washing clothes, use cold water for rinsing?   _____   _____

13. use small appliances for cooking rather than the range
    whenever possible?   _____   _____

14. open and close the refrigerator door as little as possible?   _____   _____

15. use dishwashers and washing machines with full loads?   _____   _____

16. use a clothesline to dry clothes whenever possible?   _____   _____

17. wear layered clothing in the winter and lightweight clothing
    in the summer?   _____   _____

18. change air filters on furnaces and air conditioners often?   _____   _____

19. look at EnergyGuide labels on appliances to compare costs
    when making purchasing decisions?   _____   _____

20. use public transportation whenever possible?   _____   _____

(Continued)

Choose three questions to which you responded *No*. Write plans to help your family improve in these areas.

21. Question # _____ : _____

_____

_____

_____

22. Question # _____ : _____

_____

_____

_____

23. Question # _____ : _____

_____

_____

_____

Computers in the Home

Name _____

Date _____ **Period** _____

You can use personal computers to perform many functions in the home. Working in a small group, see how many home uses for computers you can list in the computer screen below. See which group can come up with the most ideas.

Uses for Computers in the Home

Your Home of the Future

Activity B

Lesson 6-3

Name _____

Date _____ **Period** _____

Read the following story. Then answer the questions at the end of the story.

Picture yourself living in the future. You are in your early 20s and have the job of your dreams. You are single and live alone in a one-bedroom loft apartment close to where you work.

You work from 8:00 a.m. until 3:00 p.m. Work hours are shorter than they used to be. At 2:55 p.m., you phone your home computer and state that you will be arriving home shortly. You would like the air conditioning temperature lowered, your juice on ice, your favorite disc playing, and your mail ready.

You arrive home at 3:10 p.m. You open the door after you have entered the correct numbers to your computerized door lock and security system. Your robot greets you at the door with your juice. You hear the requested music playing on your disc player.

You check your computer for your electronic mail. You have a letter from your mother asking you to come to dinner this Sunday. You reply right away to her computer that you have other plans. She responds and asks you to visit on Friday. Because you work only four days a week, you agree to the visit.

You need to pay a few of your bills. You call up your bank statement on your computer to make sure you have enough money to pay your bills. You then pay your bills using your computer. It is linked by telephone lines to your bank and the places where you do business.

You are very health conscious and work out every other night. Before you go to the gym, you put your dinner in your microwave oven and program the cooking instructions. You also instruct your home robot to set the table and fix your salad.

After a workout and dinner, you decide to relax by watching a good movie. You have trouble deciding what to watch—you only have 150 choices. You decide to spend an hour on your computer learning to speak Italian instead. Following your lesson with the computer, you decide to watch an Italian TV show to check your understanding.

It is Wednesday and you always do your grocery shopping on Wednesdays. You call in your shopping list to your favorite food store through your computer. You ask for a list of specials to consult before you make your final selection. Within 15 minutes, your groceries are delivered. You instruct your home robot to put the groceries away.

1. Name three examples of technology described in this story. _____

   _____

   _____

   _____

2. List three uses of the computer mentioned in this story. _____

   _____

   _____

   _____

3. List three technological advances described in this story that are already available today. _____

   _____

   _____

Topic 7 The Foods You Eat

Food and Traditions

Activity A

Lesson 7-1

Name _____

Date _____ **Period** _____

List a food you associate with each of the holidays and special events listed below. Then answer the questions at the bottom of the page.

Holidays/Special Events	Food
New Year's Eve	_____
Graduation	_____
Fourth of July	_____
Thanksgiving	_____
Birthday	_____
Wedding	_____

1. What is a holiday, other than those listed above, that your family celebrates? _____

   _____

   How is food involved in the celebration of this holiday? _____

   _____

   _____

   What other traditions are involved in your family celebration of this holiday? _____

   _____

   _____

   How has the celebration of this holiday changed over the years? _____

   _____

   _____

2. What is a special event, other than those listed above, that your family celebrates? _____

   _____

   How is food involved in the celebration of this special event? _____

   _____

   What other traditions are involved in your family celebration of this special event? _____

   _____

   _____

   How has the celebration of this special event changed over the years? _____

   _____

   _____

Healthy Eating Checklist

Activity B

Lesson 7-1

Name _____

Date _____ Period _____

Read the list of statements below and check all those that apply to you. The more statements you check, the more closely you follow the Dietary Guidelines for Americans. After completing the checklist, fill in the "I Resolve" declaration at the bottom of the page. List all the healthful eating habits you would like to adopt.

_____ I eat a variety of foods each day.

_____ I maintain a healthy weight.

_____ I exercise regularly.

_____ I choose lean meats and trim visible fat from meat.

_____ I remove the skin from poultry before eating it.

_____ I choose fat free or lowfat milk, yogurt, and cheese most of the time.

_____ I limit the number of eggs I eat.

_____ I use fats and oils sparingly.

_____ I limit fried foods in my diet.

_____ I eat three or more servings of various vegetables every day.

_____ I eat two or more servings of various fruits every day.

_____ I choose whole grain bread and cereal products.

_____ I limit foods high in sugar.

_____ I limit foods high in salt.

I Resolve . . . .

Nutrient Chart

Name _____

Date _____ Period _____

Complete the following chart by listing the functions and food sources of each nutrient.

Nutrient	Functions	Food Sources
Proteins		
Carbohydrates		
Fats		
Vitamins		
Minerals		
Water		

Build the Pyramid

Name _____

Date _____ **Period** _____

Label the outline of the Food Guide Pyramid below. Place the name of each food group in the blank provided. Fill in the correct range of recommended daily servings for each group. Then determine the group in which each of the foods listed below belongs. Put the letter beside each food in the appropriate space in the Pyramid.

A. carrot
B. cantaloupe
C. noodles
D. clam strips
E. apple cider
F. candy bar
G. tortilla

H. grapes
I. onions
J. tuna
K. blueberry yogurt
L. chicken
M. maple syrup
N. strawberries

O. peanut butter
P. salad dressing
Q. cucumber
R. oatmeal
S. orange juice
T. Cheddar cheese

U. peach
V. bagel
W. fat free milk
X. butter
Y. crackers
Z. muffin

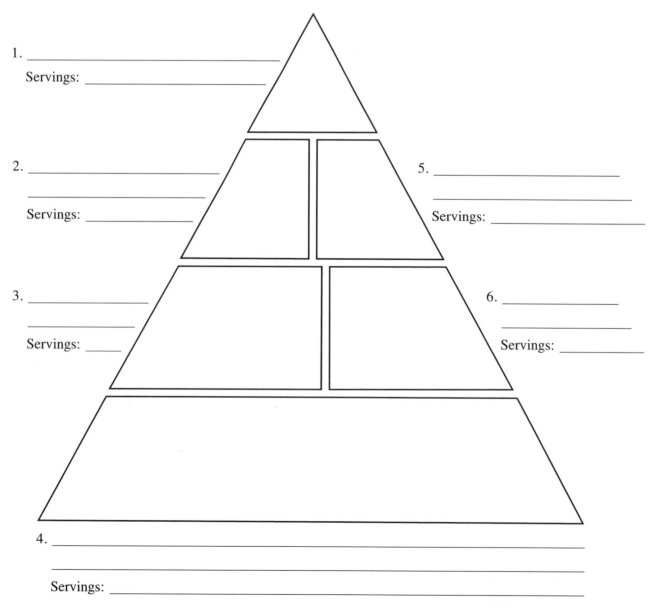

1. _____
   Servings: _____

2. _____
   _____
   Servings: _____

3. _____
   _____
   Servings: _____

4. _____
   _____
   Servings: _____

5. _____
   _____
   Servings: _____

6. _____
   _____
   Servings: _____

Little Red Vitamin Hood

Activity C

Lesson 7-2

Name _____

Date _____ Period _____

Use the following words to fill in the blanks in the story below.

A	enriched	eyes	healthy gums	nutrients
B	milk	protein	vegetables	nutrition
C	fruits	fiber	balanced diet	Food Guide Pyramid
	appearance	calcium	nervous system	

Once upon a time, there was a girl named Little Red Vitamin Hood who lived in the country. Little Red Vitamin Hood's interest in good (1)_____ was shown in her healthy (2)_____. For instance, Little Red Vitamin Hood made a point of eating plenty of dark green and yellow fruits and (3)_____. She knew they were full of vitamin (4)_____, which she needed for healthy skin and (5)_____.

One day, Little Red Vitamin Hood decided to take a nutritious lunch to her grandmother. She planned a lunch with foods from each group in the (6)_____ _____ _____. She packed roast beef for complete (7)_____. Whole grain bread would provide (8)_____. She packed oranges and strawberries from the (9)_____ group. Little Red Vitamin Hood also packed a thermos with cold (10)_____. She knew her grandmother still needed (11)_____ for strong bones, even though she was an older person.

On her way to grandmother's house, Little Red Vitamin Hood met the Big Bad Wolf. She was almost speechless with fright. She was thankful she always ate (12)_____ bread, a source of (13)_____ vitamins. She knew these vitamins helped keep her (14)_____ _____ healthy.

Little Red Vitamin Hood persuaded the Big Bad Wolf to eat an orange instead of her and her grandmother. She told him the fruit was a good source of vitamin (15)_____. This was needed for (16)_____ _____, something no self-respecting Big Bad Wolf could be without!

Little Red Vitamin Hood finally reached her grandmother's house. They ate the lunch knowing that a (17)_____ _____ would provide all the (18)_____ their bodies needed for good health.

Losing Weight

Name _____

Date _____ Period _____

The following list shows all the foods Hector ate for one day. Rewrite the list in the blanks to the right. Show how you would replace, remove, or reduce amounts of foods to help Hector lose weight. Then answer the question at the bottom of the page.

Breakfast

4 pancakes with syrup _____

2 sausage patties _____

8-ounce glass of orange juice _____

8-ounce glass of milk _____

Snack

bag of corn chips _____

Lunch

double cheeseburger _____

large order of French fries _____

12-ounce glass of cola _____

3 chocolate chip cookies _____

Snack

candy bar _____

Dinner

8-ounce steak _____

2 cups of mashed potatoes _____

1 cup green beans _____

2 wheat rolls with butter _____

8-ounce glass of milk _____

1 slice of apple pie _____

Snack

1 doughnut _____

What are three tips you would give Hector to help him plan his diet?

1. _____
   _____

2. _____
   _____

3. _____
   _____

Fad Diet Analysis

Name _____

Date _____ Period _____

Answer the following questions based on the fad diet described below.

LOSE 20 POUNDS IN JUST THREE WEEKS!
with the
AMAZING MARSHMALLOW DIET!

- This diet is simple! You don't have to count calories. Simply eat a 10-ounce bag of marshmallows each day, and you'll consume only 900 calories.

- This diet is tasty and satisfying! No more denying yourself the sweets you crave—you get to eat marshmallows all day long! You'll never go hungry! You'll be surprised how filling marshmallows can be.

- This diet has variety! Choose regular or miniature marshmallows. Eat them plain or toasted. The choice is yours!

SEND NOW for your AMAZING MARSHMALLOW DIET GUIDE. It's ONLY $34.95, and it includes dozens of helpful dieting tips to help you become
LIGHT AS A MARSHMALLOW!

---

1. How much weight does this diet promise you'll lose? _____

2. What appealing features does this diet advertise? _____

   _____

   _____

3. How many calories are allowed each day? _____

4. What food groups are excluded from this diet? _____

   _____

   _____

   _____

5. What nutrients are excluded from this diet? _____

   _____

6. Is too much of one nutrient recommended? If so, which one? _____

7. What is the fee for this diet? _____

8. Would you recommend this diet? Explain why or why not. _____

   _____

   _____

Nutrition Editor

Name _____

Date _____ Period _____

Pretend you are the nutrition editor for your local newspaper. In the spaces provided, write responses to the following letters readers have sent into your weekly column, "Calorie Corner."

1. *Dear Calorie Corner,*

    "Low-calorie dessert recipes," "Reduced-calorie salad dressing," "1200-calorie diet plan"—the word "calorie" seems to be everywhere. What exactly are calories? Do we really need them?

    Signed,
    Hungry for Information

    Dear Hungry,

    _____

    _____

    _____

2. *Dear Calorie Corner,*

    I'm a 12-year-old girl. My doctor told me I should be eating about 2,200 calories per day. The doctor told my 15-year-old brother he could eat 3,000 calories per day. Why is my brother allowed to eat more than I am?

    Signed,
    Snack Happy

    Dear Snack,

    _____

    _____

    _____

3. *Dear Calorie Corner,*

    I'm on the football team at school. My coach told me I'm going to need to gain five pounds before the season starts. Do you have any tips to help me gain weight?

    Signed,
    Lightweight

    Dear Lightweight,

    _____

    _____

    _____

4. *Dear Calorie Corner,*

    I like to spend most of my spare time reading. My mom says I don't get enough exercise. What can exercise do for me anyway?

    Signed,
    Bookworm

    Dear Bookworm,

    _____

    _____

    _____

Topic 8 Planning Meals

Planning Pointers

Activity A

Lesson 8-1

Name _____

Date _____ **Period** _____

Each of the following statements refers to a point you should keep in mind when planning menus. In the column on the right, write the points in the blanks using the words below. After each statement, give an example of how the point affects foods served in your home.

convenience	family customs	taste
cost	nutrition	variety
culture		

Planning Point

1. In Jamie's home, bagels and cocoa are served for breakfast every Sunday Morning.

    _____ _____

    _____

2. Justine wants to be sure she gets all the vitamins and minerals she needs without eating too much fat.

    _____ _____

    _____

3. Ramone enjoys the flavor of pork chops.

    _____ _____

    _____

4. Carmelita's mother is from Mexico and often serves tacos, burritos, and other Mexican foods.

    _____ _____

    _____

5. Keisha likes foods that are easy and quick to prepare.

    _____ _____

    _____

6. Amad likes rice, but he would not want to eat it every day.

    _____ _____

    _____

7. Lemuel shops for food that fits into the family's food budget.

    _____ _____

    _____

A Meal with Appeal

Name _____

Date _____ **Period** _____

Cut a picture of a meal from a magazine and mount it in the space below. Then answer the questions that follow based on what you see in the picture.

1. What type of meal is this? _____

2. In the first column below, write the meal pattern given in the text for this type of meal. In the second column, indicate which food in the picture represents each item in the meal pattern.

   _____   _____

   _____   _____

   _____   _____

   _____   _____

   _____   _____

3. How does this meal include a variety of colors? _____

   _____

4. How does this meal include a variety of shapes? _____

   _____

5. How does this meal include a variety of flavors? _____

   _____

6. How does this meal include a variety of textures? _____

   _____

7. How does this meal include a variety of temperatures? _____

   _____

8. If you were serving this meal, what, if anything, would you change about it? _____

   _____

Secrets to Shopping Skillfully

Activity A

Lesson 8-2

Name _____

Date _____ Period _____

The following sentences are food shopping tips from the lesson. Each sentence contains a coded word. Use the example and the tips to break the code. Then decode the shopping secret at the bottom of the page.

Example: <u>S H O P</u>   <u>S M A R T</u>
        G F N O   G A B X J

1. Shop when you are not __ __ __ __ __ __ .
           F P S I X R (hungry)

2. When there are __ __ __ __ __ __ __ __ __ , food prices go up.
           G F N X J B I W G (shortages)

3. Larger packages may be better __ __ __ __ __ __ than small packages.
           K B M P W G (values)

4. Buy only what is on your shopping __ __ __ __ .
           M L G J (list)

5. List foods on your shopping list in the __ __ __ __ __ they are found in the store.
           N X Y W X (order)

6. Compare the prices, quality, and __ __ __ __ __ __ __ of foods in each type of store.
           K B X L W J R (variety)

7. Look for a store that has well-packaged foods with __ __ __ __ __ __ clearly marked.
           O X L T W G (prices)

8. Look at the price and weight of each product and __ __ __ __ __ __ __ what each has to offer.
           T N A O B X W (compare)

9. Choose packages that give the best __ __ __ __ __ __ __ food at the price you want to pay.
           D P B M L J R (quality)

10. Read the __ __ __ __ __ __ on packages.
            M B E W M G (labels)

Shopping Secret: __ __ __   __ __ __   __ __ __ __ __   __ <u>K</u> __ __ __ __
        R N P   T B S   M W B X S   G Z L M M G

__ __   __ __ __ __ __ __   __ <u>W</u> __ __ __ __   __ __   __ __ __
J N   E W T N A W   B Q L S S W X   B J   J F W

<u>F</u> __ __ __   __ __ __ __ __ __ __ __   __ __ __ __
H N N Y   G F N O O L S I   I B A W

Read the Label

Activity B

Lesson 8-2

Name _____

Date _____ Period _____

Use the nutrition label below to answer the questions that follow.

Nutrition Facts

Serving Size 1 cup (240mL)
Servings Per Container 8

Amount Per Serving

Calories 120   Calories from Fat 0

% Daily Value*

Total Fat 0g	**0%**
Saturated Fat 0g	**0%**
Cholesterol 0mg	**0%**
Sodium 0mg	**0%**
Total Carbohydrate 28g	**9%**
Dietary Fiber 1g	**4%**
Sugars 24g	
Protein 2g	

Vitamin A 4% **Vitamin C** 130%
Calcium 2%   **Iron** 1%

Percent Daily Values are based on a 2,000 calorie diet. Your daily values may be higher or lower depending on your calorie needs:

	Calories	2,000	2,500
Total Fat	less than	65g	80g
Sat Fat	less than	20g	25g
Cholesterol	less than	300mg	300mg
Sodium	less than	2,400mg	2,400mg
Total Carbohydrate		300g	375g
Dietary Fiber		25g	30g

Calories per gram:
Fat 9 • Carbohydrates 4 • Protein 4

1. What is the serving size for this product?

_____

2. How many servings are in the product package?

_____

3. How many calories are in a serving of this product?

_____

4. What is the first nutrient listed on the label?

_____

5. How much sodium is in a serving of this product?

_____

6. What percent of the Daily Value for total carbohydrate does a serving of this product provide?

_____

7. How much dietary fiber does a serving of this product provide?

_____

8. How much protein does a serving of this product provide?

_____

9. What percent of the Daily Value for vitamin C does a serving of this product provide?

_____

10. How many total grams of carbohydrate should be consumed each day by someone on a 2,500-calorie diet?

_____

11. **Extra Credit**

How many calories per serving come from carbohydrates?

_____

Shopping Carefully

Name _____

Date _____ Period _____

Write three hints to keep in mind when buying foods from each of the major food groups.

1. What should you keep in mind when buying fruits?

    a. _____

    b. _____

    c. _____

2. What should you keep in mind when buying vegetables?

    a. _____

    b. _____

    c. _____

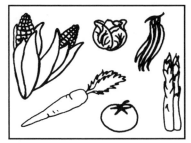

3. What should you keep in mind when buying bread, cereal, rice, and pasta?

    a. _____

    b. _____

    c. _____

4. What should you keep in mind when buying milk, yogurt, and cheese?

    a. _____

    b. _____

    c. _____

5. What should you keep in mind when buying meat, poultry, fish, dry beans, eggs, and nuts?

    a. _____

    b. _____

    c. _____

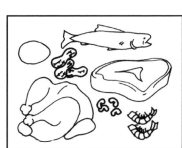

Home from the Store

William has just returned from the supermarket. Help him unpack and store the food. Write the name of each food in the correct storage area of the kitchen.

pork chops

eggs

fat free milk

ice cream

rye bread

celery

hamburger buns

potatoes

rice

dried navy beans

yogurt

nonfat dry milk

frozen orange juice

apples

canned corn

evaporated milk

frozen spinach

canned tuna

hot dogs

canned peas

lettuce

cheddar cheese

whole wheat flour

grapes

Setting Pretty

Activity A

Lesson 8-4

Name _____

Date _____ **Period** _____

Look at the place setting below. In the space provided, list what is incorrect about the place setting. Then draw a picture of a correct place setting.

What are four things that are wrong with this place setting?

a. _____

b. _____

c. _____

d. _____

Draw a correct place setting for this menu.

Table Service Crossword

Name _____

Date _____ Period _____

Use the text information on table setting and meal service to fill in the blanks. Then complete the crossword puzzle.

Across

_____ 1. A formal meal for a special event may require a more complex table _____.

_____ 2. _____ include plates, bowls, mugs, cups, and saucers.

_____ 3. A _____ is a decorative object placed in the middle of the table.

_____ 7. _____ service is a style of meal service where plates are filled in the kitchen and then served at the table.

_____ 8. Forks, knives, and spoons used for serving and eating are called _____.

_____ 9. _____ includes all types of drinking glasses.

_____ 10. _____ service is a style of meal service where people help themselves to food set out on a serving table.

Down

_____ 1. Family, buffet, and plate are all styles of meal _____.

_____ 4. _____ is dishes, flatware, and glassware.

_____ 5. A _____ is the table space in front of a person's seat.

_____ 6. _____ service is a style of meal service where people serve themselves as dishes are passed around the table.

What Should You Do?

Name _____

Date _____ Period _____

Think about the importance of good table manners. Then write the correct way to handle each situation described below.

1. You need to cut the pork chop on your plate into bite-size pieces. _____
   _____

2. You are eating in a friend's home, and you would like some more salad. The salad is in a bowl at the other end of the table. _____
   _____
   _____

3. You wish to eat the bowl of tomato soup your waiter has just placed in front of you. _____
   _____
   _____

4. You have spilled your drink while eating at a friend's home. _____
   _____
   _____

5. You have finished your meal at an FHA banquet and need to put down the flatware you are holding. ____
   _____
   _____

6. You are attending a picnic in your aunt's backyard. You want to eat some of the fried chicken she has served. _____
   _____
   _____

7. Your family has gathered around the table for dinner. Your father is not yet seated. _____
   _____
   _____

8. You are eating lunch at a friend's home. Your friend has served mashed potatoes, which you do not like.
   _____
   _____

9. You have a meeting after dinner and need to leave the table as soon as you have finished eating. _____
   _____
   _____

10. You are in a restaurant where they serve homemade whole wheat bread. You want to eat your bread with butter. _____
    _____
    _____

Entertaining at Home

Name _____

Date _____ **Period** _____

Answer the following questions as a guide to help you plan an event in your home.

1. What type of event will this be? _____

2. When will you hold this event? _____

3. How many people will you invite? _____

4. How and when will you invite your guests? _____

5. How will you prepare your home for this event? _____

   _____

   _____

6. What types of food will you serve? _____

   _____

   _____

7. How will you decorate for this event? _____

   _____

   _____

8. What types of activities will you plan to entertain your guests? _____

   _____

   _____

9. What will you need to buy before the event? _____

   _____

10. Who will help you prepare for this event? _____

    _____

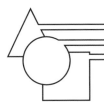

Topic 9 You in the Kitchen

Appliance Use and Care

Activity A

Lesson 9-1

Name _____

Date _____ **Period** _____

Choose one of the large appliances in your school foods lab. Get the use and care manual for your chosen appliance from your teacher. Use the manual to fill in the information requested below.

Appliance: _____

Brand: _____

Model: _____

Purpose: _____

Features: _____

_____

_____

_____

_____

Cleaning guidelines:

_____

_____

_____

_____

Safety tips:

_____

_____

_____

_____

Where and how to repair:

_____

_____

Other information included in the manual:

_____

_____

Tool Hunt

Activity B

Lesson 9-1

Name _____

Date _____ Period _____

Find the following tools in your school foods lab. Write down the location and purpose of each tool.

blender

1. Location: _____

   Purpose: _____

slow cooker

5. Location: _____

   Purpose: _____

toaster

2. Location: _____

   Purpose: _____

saucepan

6. Location: _____

   Purpose: _____

electric skillet

3. Location: _____

   Purpose: _____

pot

7. Location: _____

   Purpose: _____

electric mixer

4. Location: _____

   Purpose: _____

skillet

8. Location: _____

   Purpose: _____

(Continued)

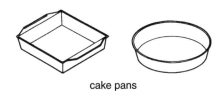

cake pans

9. Location: _____

   Purpose: _____

cookie sheet

13. Location: _____

   Purpose: _____

pie pan

10. Location: _____

   Purpose: _____

roasting pan with rack

14. Location: _____

   Purpose: _____

pizza pan

11. Location: _____

   Purpose: _____

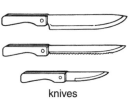

knives

15. Location: _____

   Purpose: _____

muffin pan

12. Location: _____

   Purpose: _____

cutting board

16. Location: _____

   Purpose: _____

(Continued)

spatula

17. Location: _____

Purpose: _____

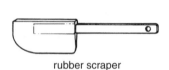

rubber scraper

18. Location: _____

Purpose: _____

wooden spoon

19. Location: _____

Purpose: _____

mixing bowls

20. Location: _____

Purpose: _____

measuring spoon

21. Location: _____

Purpose: _____

colander

22. Location: _____

Purpose: _____

dry measuring
cups

23. Location: _____

Purpose: _____

liquid
measuring cup

24. Location: _____

Purpose: _____

Find the Dangers!

Study the picture of the kitchen below. List eight unsafe conditions you see. Then give four suggestions that would improve the safety in this kitchen.

Unsafe conditions:

1. _____
2. _____
3. _____
4. _____
5. _____
6. _____
7. _____
8. _____

Suggestions for improvement:

1. _____
2. _____
3. _____
4. _____

Cleanup Strip

Activity B

Lesson 9-2

Name _____

Date _____ Period _____

Develop a filmstrip on kitchen cleanliness. Illustrate five cleaning guidelines and write what should be said beside each drawing.

_____

_____

_____

_____

_____

_____

_____

_____

_____

_____

_____

_____

_____

_____

_____

_____

_____

_____

_____

_____

_____

_____

_____

Following Directions

Activity A   **Name** _____

Lesson 9-3   **Date** _____ **Period** _____

Using recipes successfully requires you to follow directions carefully. This is an exercise to see how well you can follow directions. Read everything on this page before you begin. Then follow the directions.

1. Write your name and the date and period in the space provided.

2. Put a star in the top left-hand corner of this page.

3. Draw a circle around the star.

4. Stand up and sit back down.

5. Write the number 100 in the top right-hand corner of this page.

6. Draw a smiling face beside the 100.

7. Pat your back.

8. Say your name out loud.

9. Write the abbreviations for the following words:

   Ounce: _____

   Cup: _____

   Tablespoon: _____

   Pound: _____

10. Write the name of your favorite food. _____

11. Write the name of your favorite restaurant. _____

    _____

12. Say out loud, "I am almost finished."

13. Now that you have read everything on this page, do step 1 and ignore the other steps.

Follow Me

Name _____

Date _____ Period _____

Read the recipe. Then answer the questions below.

Blueberry Muffins
(Makes 12 muffins)

1 egg	2 tablespoons sugar
1 cup milk	2 ½ teaspoons baking powder
¼ cup oil	½ teaspoon salt
2 cups flour	¾ cup blueberries

1. Preheat oven to 400°F.
2. Grease bottoms of 12 medium muffin cups.
3. In a medium mixing bowl, beat egg; stir in milk and oil.
4. In a small mixing bowl, combine flour, sugar, baking powder, and salt.
5. Add dry ingredients to liquid ingredients. Stir just until flour is moistened. Batter should be lumpy.
6. Fold blueberries into batter.
7. Fill muffin cups two-thirds full.
8. Bake for 20-25 minutes until golden brown.
9. Remove from pan. Serve warm.

1. What food product does this recipe make? _____

2. How many ingredients are needed? _____

3. Which ingredient is needed in the largest amount? _____

4. What are two preparation tasks that must be done before mixing the ingredients? _____

   _____

5. What are the mixing directions? _____

   _____

   _____

   _____

6. What is the baking temperature? _____

7. How long does this food need to bake? _____

8. How many servings will this recipe make? _____

9. Write any words used in this recipe you do not understand. _____

   _____

Measuring Tools Match

Name _____

Date _____ Period _____

Match each ingredient in Column A with the measuring tool(s) in Column B you would use to measure it.

Column A

_____ 1. 1 cup milk

_____ 2. 2 teaspoons vanilla

_____ 3. ½ cup shortening

_____ 4. ⅔ cup sugar

_____ 5. 1 tablespoon water

_____ 6. ¼ teaspoon cinnamon

_____ 7. ¼ cup orange juice

_____ 8. 1½ teaspoons baking soda

_____ 9. ½ cup maple syrup

_____ 10. 1 cup chocolate chips

_____ 11. ¼ cup brown sugar

_____ 12. ⅓ cup flour

Column B

a.  1 T.

b.  1 c.

c.  1 t.

d. ◻ ⅓ c.

e. ◻ ⅓ c.   ◻ ⅓ c.

f. 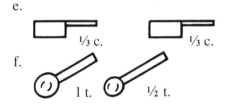 1 t.   ½ t.

g. ◻ ¼ c.

h. ◻ ¼ c.

i. ◻ ½ c.

j. ◻ 1 c.

k. ◻ ¼ t.

l. ◻ ½ c.

The Cutting Board

Name _____

Date _____ Period _____

Fill in the blanks with the correct cutting terms. Then complete the crossword puzzle.

Across

_____ 1. To divide foods into small pieces.

_____ 4. To cut food into very small pieces with a sharp knife or kitchen shears.

_____ 6. To rub a food back and forth against a grater to get very small pieces.

_____ 7. To remove the skin of a food using a paring knife.

Down

_____ 1. To cut food in small, even cubes.

_____ 2. To cut food into even pieces using a knife.

_____ 3. To remove the center of a food, such as an apple.

_____ 5. To cut food into small pieces using a sharp knife, food processor, or blender.

Making More or Less

Activity C

Lesson 9-4

Name _____

Date _____ Period _____

Practice your recipe math. First double the yield and ingredients in the following recipe. Then cut the recipe in half.

Raisin Nut Oatmeal Cookies

Double Recipe		Half Recipe
1. _____	(Makes about 4 dozen medium-sized cookies)	_____
2. _____	2 eggs	_____
3. _____	1 cup brown sugar	_____
4. _____	1 cup oil	_____
5. _____	¼ cup molasses	_____
6. _____	3 tablespoons milk	_____
7. _____	2 cups flour	_____
8. _____	½ teaspoon salt	_____
9. _____	1 teaspoon baking soda	_____
10. _____	1 teaspoon cinnamon	_____
11. _____	½ teaspoon ginger, cloves, and nutmeg	_____
12. _____	½ cup raisins (softened in water and drained)	_____
13. _____	½ cup chopped nuts	_____
14. _____	2¼ cups quick rolled oats	_____

Note: If you wish to make this recipe at home or in your school foods lab, use the following directions:

1. Preheat oven to 325°F.
2. Beat eggs well in a large mixing bowl.
3. Add brown sugar and beat until well blended.
4. Slowly pour in oil. Mix well.
5. Add molasses and milk. Blend well.
6. Mix together flour, salt, baking soda, and spices.
7. Add to mixture along with raisins and nuts. Mix just to blend.
8. Add oats and stir lightly.
9. Drop from a teaspoon on ungreased baking sheet.
10. Bake 20 minutes or until light brown.

Mixing and Cooking Crossword

Activity A

Lesson 9-5

Name _____

Date _____ Period _____

Use the text information on mixing and cooking terms to fill in the blanks. Then complete the crossword puzzle.

Across

_____ 3. To heat a liquid on a range at a high temperature.

_____ 6. To cook in fat or oil in a pan.

_____ 9. To allow food to finish cooking by internal heat after being removed from a microwave oven.

_____ 10. To beat a mixture until it is light and fluffy using a spoon or electric mixer.

_____ 13. To beat quickly using a wire whisk or rotary beater to add air to one or more ingredients.

_____ 14. To cook by direct heat under the broiling unit in an oven or on a barbecue grill.

_____ 15. To mix fast bringing the contents to the top of the bowl and then back down again.

(Continued)

Down

_____ 1. To mix two or more ingredients together using a spoon.

_____ 2. To mix slowly using a spoon or an electric mixer on low speed.

_____ 4. To mix solid shortening into a flour mixture using two knives or a pastry blender to cut through the shortening.

_____ 5. To cook small pieces of food in a small amount of fat, stirring often.

_____ 6. To cook uncovered in an oven without liquid.

_____ 7. To cook in a microwave oven.

_____ 8. To cook in a liquid at just below the boiling point.

_____ 9. To mix in a circular motion using a spoon.

_____ 10. To mix a light, airy substance with a more solid substance by folding the two together with a rubber scraper.

_____ 14. To cook in an oven in an uncovered container.

Mixing Terms in Recipes

Name _____

Date _____ Period _____

Find examples of recipes that use each of the mixing terms in the chart below. Complete the chart by writing down the name of the recipe. Also list the tool you would use for the specified mixing method. Then list the ingredients that are being mixed by each method.

Mixing Method	Recipe	Tool	Ingredients
Beat			
Blend			
Combine			
Fold			
Cream			
Stir			
Cut in			
Whip			

Food Preparation Study Guide

Name _____

Date _____ Period _____

Using information in the lesson, write the letter of the answer that best completes each statement in the space provided.

_____ 1. Fresh fruits should be _____ before eating.
A. washed
B. cut

_____ 2. To prevent fruits such as apples or bananas from turning brown after you slice them, dip the slices in _____.
A. water
B. lemon or orange juice

_____ 3. Frozen fruit should be thawed _____ before serving.
A. fully
B. slightly

_____ 4. To help fruit hold its shape, cook it for a short amount of time and add _____.
A. sugar
B. gelatin

_____ 5. Cook vegetables until they are _____.
A. soft
B. tender but crisp

_____ 6. Use a _____ amount of water when cooking vegetables.
A. small
B. large

_____ 7. Frozen vegetables should be cooked _____.
A. after they have been thawed
B. while they are still frozen

_____ 8. Dry vegetables need to be cooked for a _____ amount of time than other vegetables.
A. shorter
B. longer

_____ 9. _____ is thick and needs to be rolled before baking.
A. Dough
B. Batter

_____ 10. Both batter and dough include a _____ agent that causes them to rise during baking.
A. rising
B. leavening

_____ 11. Muffins, biscuits, nut breads, and pancakes are examples of _____ breads.
A. quick
B. yeast

_____ 12. _____ and baking powder are the leavening agents added to quick breads.
A. Yeast
B. Baking soda

_____ 13. Yeast breads take _____ time to make than quick breads.
A. more
B. less

(Continued)

_____ 14. Cereals, such as pasta and rice, _____ when cooked.
  A. expand
  B. shrink

_____ 15. _____ wash rice before or after cooking.
  A. Do
  B. Do not

_____ 16. When cooking cereal, if the temperature is too _____ the cereal can become tough or lumpy.
  A. low
  B. high

_____ 17. _____ temperatures can cause milk to curdle.
  A. Low
  B. High

_____ 18. Film that forms on top of heated milk _____ dissolve.
  A. will
  B. will not

_____ 19. Overcooking cheese makes it _____.
  A. soft and runny
  B. tough and rubbery

_____ 20. Cheese will be less likely to overcook and will melt faster if it is _____.
  A. left in a large chunk
  B. cut into small pieces

_____ 21. Moist heat cooking methods are best for _____ protein foods.
  A. less tender
  B. tender

_____ 22. Roasting, baking, broiling, grilling, and frying are _____ heat cooking methods.
  A. moist
  B. dry

_____ 23. If eggs are _____, they become tough and rubbery.
  A. undercooked
  B. overcooked

_____ 24. The rich flavor of desserts often comes from _____.
  A. milk and eggs
  B. fat and sugar

Food Preparation Demonstration

Activity B

Lesson 9-6

Name _____

Date _____ **Period** _____

Choose a simple recipe to demonstrate to the class. Your recipe should use one of the food preparation techniques covered in the lesson. Write your recipe in the space provided. Then answer the questions below to help you prepare your demonstration talk.

Name of recipe: _____

Ingredients needed: (Specify the amount of each ingredient.)

_____   _____

_____   _____

_____   _____

_____   _____

Directions: _____

_____

_____

_____

Cooking time: _____

Cooking temperature: _____

Number of servings: _____

1. What type of food are you preparing? _____

2. What nutrients does this food contribute to the diet? _____

3. What preparation technique will you be demonstrating? _____

4. What guidelines should you follow that will help your food product turn out right? _____

_____

_____

5. At what type of meal might you serve the food product you are making? _____

6. What other foods might be served with this food product? _____

_____

7. Why did you choose to demonstrate this recipe? _____

_____

8. List any other points you want to mention during your demonstration. _____

_____

_____

_____

Easing Meal Preparation

Name _____

Date _____ Period _____

Read the following case studies. Then give a suggestion that would help make meal preparation easier in each situation.

1. Domingo is baby-sitting his little brother. He wants to make chili for them for supper. He reads over his mother's recipe and checks to be sure he has all the ingredients. The recipe makes six servings. Domingo decides to make a third of a recipe since he needs only two servings. What meal preparation suggestion would you tell Domingo to follow the next time he is cooking for two?

_____

_____

_____

2. This morning, Issac's parents told him he could make whatever he wanted for dinner. He planned to make roast chicken, double-baked potatoes, and salad with homemade dressing. After spending the day picking up litter, delivering papers, and shooting baskets, Issac started cooking. He got the chicken in the oven and then looked at his watch. Issac realized it was time to meet his friends for a movie. He never had time to finish preparing his fancy dinner, much less eat it! What meal preparation suggestion would you tell Issac to follow the next time his schedule is so full?

_____

_____

_____

3. Karina is preparing leftover soup for lunch. She empties the soup from the storage container into a pan on the range. When it is hot, Karina pours the soup into a large serving bowl. At the table, Karina fills individual soup bowls from the serving bowl. What suggestion would you give Karina to help make meal preparation easier?

_____

_____

_____

4. Tamica is in charge of getting dinner ready before her parents get home from work. She never thinks about what she is going to serve until she gets home from school. Then she opens a cookbook, picks a recipe, and starts cooking. Sometimes Tamica gets something halfway mixed and then realizes she is missing some ingredients. When this happens, Tamica adapts the recipe with whatever she has on hand. That's how she ended up serving pineapple lasagna last week! What meal preparation suggestion would you give Tamica to help her avoid serving such strange foods in the future?

_____

_____

_____

Kitchen Organization

Name _____

Date _____ Period _____

Write the name of each item under the work center where it should be stored.

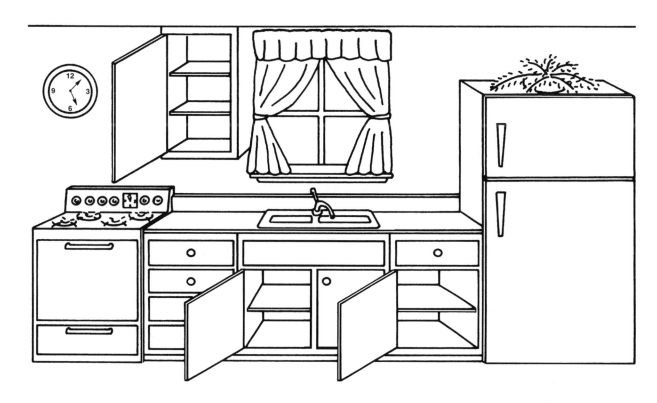

Preparation and Serving Area	Cleanup Area	Food Storage Area
_____	_____	_____
_____	_____	_____
_____	_____	_____
_____	_____	_____
_____	_____	_____
_____	_____	_____
dish detergent	cutting board	forks and spoons
potholders	skillet	dish towel
plastic wrap	cookie sheet	ice cream scoop
saucepans	measuring spoons	ice tongs
foil	dishes and glassware	knives
plastic containers	muffin pan	canned foods

School Foods Lab Work Plan

Name _____

Date _____ Period _____

In small groups, write a work plan for preparing the recipe on this page. Follow the guidelines below to complete the work plan on the following page.

1. Attach a copy of your recipe to your work plan.

2. Read your recipe carefully. In the spaces at the bottom of this page, list the tools you need for measuring, cutting, mixing, and cooking.

3. On a separate sheet of paper, list any advance preparation tasks. These tasks might include gathering tools and ingredients, boiling water, melting shortening, greasing pans, chopping onions, and preheating the oven.

4. On the same sheet of paper, list measuring, mixing, and cooking tasks needed to prepare the recipe.

5. List serving and cleanup tasks, including setting the table.

6. Beside each task on your list, write an estimate of how many minutes it will take to do the task.

7. Determine the order in which tasks should be completed. Rewrite your task list in this order in the *Task* column on the work plan sheet.

8. Use your estimates from Step 6 to decide when tasks should be started. Write these times in the *Time* column on your work plan sheet.

9. Identify the person who will be responsible for each task in the *Group Member* column on your work plan sheet. Be sure the work is evenly divided.

10. Make copies of your work plan for everyone in your group. Be sure everyone knows who is responsible for performing each task.

Mini Pizzas
(Makes 6 mini pizzas)

6 refrigerated biscuits	
⅓ cup tomato paste	½ teaspoon oregano
2 tablespoons water	dash of pepper
1 teaspoon oil	½ cup grated mozzarella cheese
¼ teaspoon garlic salt	2 tablespoons Parmesan cheese

1. Preheat the oven to 425°F.
2. Lightly grease a cookie sheet.
3. Spread the dough of each biscuit out with your fingers on the cookie sheet so you have six crusts. With your fingers, make a raised edge on each crust.
4. In a small bowl, mix the tomato paste, water, oil, garlic salt, oregano, and pepper together.
5. Spread a few teaspoons of sauce on each crust.
6. Top each pizza with grated mozzarella and Parmesan cheese.
7. Bake for 8-10 minutes until brown.

Tools needed:

_____ _____

_____ _____

_____ _____

Name _____

Lab number _____

Date _____

Period _____

Lab group assignments

Cook _____

Assistant cook _____

Host/Food server _____

_____

Work Plan

Time	Task	Group Member

School Foods Lab Evaluation

Activity B

Lesson 9-8

Name _____

Date _____ Period _____

Answer the following questions about your experience in the school foods lab. Check either the *Yes* column or the *No* column and add up your points. Then answer the questions at the bottom of the page.

	Yes	No
Did I	_____	_____
1. participate in the planning of the work plan for my group?	_____	_____
2. come to class prepared?	_____	_____
3. begin to work right away?	_____	_____
4. pull my hair back, if necessary? (Check *yes* if you have short hair.)	_____	_____
5. wear an apron?	_____	_____
6. wash my hands before I started to cook?	_____	_____
7. read the recipe carefully before I started to cook?	_____	_____
8. get out all ingredients before I started to cook?	_____	_____
9. get out all tools before I started to cook?	_____	_____
10. use correct measuring techniques?	_____	_____
11. follow the recipe carefully?	_____	_____
12. follow the work plan set up by my group?	_____	_____
13. avoid wasting time in class?	_____	_____
14. talk only when necessary?	_____	_____
15. keep the kitchen clean as I worked?	_____	_____
16. use good table manners?	_____	_____
17. taste all foods prepared?	_____	_____
18. assist my group with the cleanup duties?	_____	_____

19. leave the school foods lab clean with all tools in the proper place?

20. leave the classroom only when the teacher dismissed me?

For each *No* response checked, subtract 5 points from 100 for your score.

Score _____

If your score was less than 90, how do you need to improve when working in the school foods lab? _____

_____

What did you learn from this school foods lab experience? _____

_____

What would you do differently if you were repeating this school foods lab experience? Explain your answer.

_____

_____

Topic 10 Buying and Caring for Clothes

Clothing Needs

Activity A

Lesson 10-1

Name _____

Date _____ Period _____

Find examples of clothes that show how the three factors—standards of dress, activities, and climate—affect your clothing needs. Cut a picture from a magazine or catalog for each factor and glue it in the space provided. Then explain why each item of clothing would be appropriate for your needs.

Standards of Dress	**Activities**
This would be good for me to wear in my community because _____ _____ _____	This would be good for me to wear because I like to _____ _____ _____

Climate

This would be good for me to wear because the weather is _____

_____

_____

Analyzing Your Wardrobe

Activity B

Lesson 10-1

Name _____

Date _____ Period _____

Take an inventory of your clothes and accessories. Then answer the questions on the next page.

Wardrobe Inventory			
List of My Clothes	**Description**	**Condition**	**Notes**
Shirts			
Sweaters			
Suits/Dresses			
Pants			
Shorts			
Undergarments			
Socks			
Shoes			
Coats			
Accessories			

(Continued)

1. Describe an item of clothing you have (other than blue jeans) that would be considered a classic. _____

    _____

    _____

2. Describe an item of clothing you have that would be considered a fad. _____

    _____

    _____

3. List two items of clothing you have that were selected because of the climate you live in. Explain why.

    _____

    _____

4. Describe an item of clothing you have that was selected because it is the standard of dress at your school.

    Explain why. _____

    _____

    _____

5. List two items of clothing you have that were selected for certain activities. _____

    _____

    _____

6. Describe items of clothing you have that you mix and match to make more outfits. _____

    _____

    _____

7. What items of clothing do you have that are in need of repair? _____

    _____

    _____

8. What clothing items did you decide to discard from your wardrobe? _____

    _____

    _____

9. Considering your wardrobe inventory, what items of clothing do you need to add to your wardrobe?

    Explain why. _____

    _____

    _____

    _____

    _____

    _____

    _____

    _____

    _____

Buying Clothes

Name _____

Date _____ Period _____

Use the text information on shopping for clothes to fill in the blanks. Then complete the crossword puzzle.

Across

_____ 2. A store that sells a limited type of goods.

_____ 4. Method of payment that transfers money from your account to the store's account.

_____ 5. Having this will make it easier to return an item.

_____ 6. Clothing offered at reduced prices.

_____ 7. Compare this to get the best buy when making clothing purchases.

_____ 8. Placing a small deposit on an item so the store will hold it for you.

_____ 9. A way to pay that lets you buy now and pay later.

Down

_____ 1. A store that sells surplus clothing and clothing that is not quite perfect. (Two words.)

_____ 3. To return an item for another item.

_____ 4. An easy way to pay for small purchases.

Shopping Behavior

Name _____

Date _____ **Period** _____

Complete each statement below describing polite customer behavior.

1. Polite behavior toward a salesclerk means I will _____
   _____
   _____

2. Polite behavior toward other customers means I will _____
   _____
   _____

3. When I need to make a complaint about an item I bought, I should _____
   _____
   _____

4. When I am pleased with the goods and services a store offers, I should _____
   _____
   _____

5. When I can't make up my mind about buying a garment, I should ask these questions about returns and exchanges: _____
   _____
   _____
   _____
   _____

6. When I am trying on a garment, I should _____
   _____
   _____

7. When I am through trying on a garment, I should _____
   _____
   _____
   _____

Hang Ten

Name _____

Date _____ Period _____

Look at the label and hangtag for the blue jeans illustrated below. Then answer the 10 questions that follow.

<table>
<tr><td>

100% cotton
made by **Rodeo King**
in the USA

machine wash in cold water
tumble dry on low heat

</td></tr>
</table>

label

Rodeo King

producers of the best blue
jeans made
preshrunk and colorfast

Waist-29/Length-28
100% cotton

satisfaction guaranteed or
your money back

Made in the U.S.A.

hangtag

1. What is the fiber content of the blue jeans? _____

2. How would you wash these blue jeans? _____

3. How should these blue jeans be dried? _____

4. What is the name of the manufacturer? _____

5. Where were these blue jeans made? _____

6. What special treatments has the fabric received to improve the fit and appearance of the blue jeans?

   _____

7. What size are the blue jeans? _____

8. Is there a special guarantee? _____ If so, what is it? _____

   _____

9. What do you think is the most helpful piece of information on the label or hangtag? _____

   _____

10. What do you think is the least helpful piece of information on the label or hangtag? _____

    _____

Label and Hangtag Design

Name _____

Date _____ Period _____

Design a label and a hangtag for the shirt below. Be sure to include all information required by law to be on labels. You may want to review page 279 of the text.

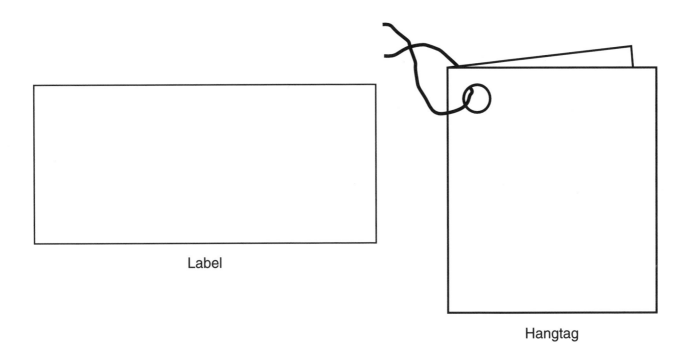

Label

Hangtag

Fiber Traits and Uses

Activity A

Lesson 10-4

Name _____

Date _____ Period _____

Complete the charts below by listing traits and uses for each fiber. Also list the source of each natural fiber.

Natural Fibers	Sources	Traits	Uses
Cotton			
Flax			
Ramie			
Wool			
Silk			

Manufactured Fibers	Traits	Uses
Rayon		
Nylon		
Acrylic		
Polyester		

Fabrics and Finishes

Name _____

Date _____ Period _____

Read the definitions and write the terms in the spaces provided. Then write a sentence explaining how the secret sentence is related to fabrics and finishes.

1. Prevents water from soaking into fabrics.
2. Prevents fabrics from shrinking.
3. Prevents fabrics from burning easily.
4. Fibers made from raw materials and chemicals.
5. Prevents fabrics from wrinkling.
6. A treatment to improve fibers, yarns, and fabrics.
7. A type of fabric made by melting fibers together.
8. A type of knit made by two sets of needles.
9. Helps soaps and detergents remove soil when washing.
10. A combination of two or more fibers.
11. Two or more yarns looped together.
12. A type of knit made from one yarn.

1. — — — — — — — — — —
2. — — — — — — — — —
3. — — — — — — — — — — — — — —
4. — — — — — — — — — — — —
5. — — — — — — — — — — — — —
6. — — — — — —
7. — — — — — — —
8. — — — — — —
9. — — — — — — — — — —
10. — — — — —
11. — — — — — —
12. — — — — —

13. What is the secret sentence? _____

14. How does the secret sentence relate to fabrics and finishes? _____

_____

_____

Sort It

Name _____

Date _____ Period _____

Below is a list of clothes that can be washed in the washing machine. Sort the clothes into wash loads by placing the letter beside the item in the correct laundry bag.

A. white cotton shirt
B. blue jeans
C. red cotton sweater
D. white sheets
E. leotards (dancing)
F. football uniform
G. white T-shirt

H. navy blue slacks
I. light tan shirt
J. black sweatshirt
K. light blue skirt
L. yellow knit shirt
M. hand knit green dress
N. dark blue socks

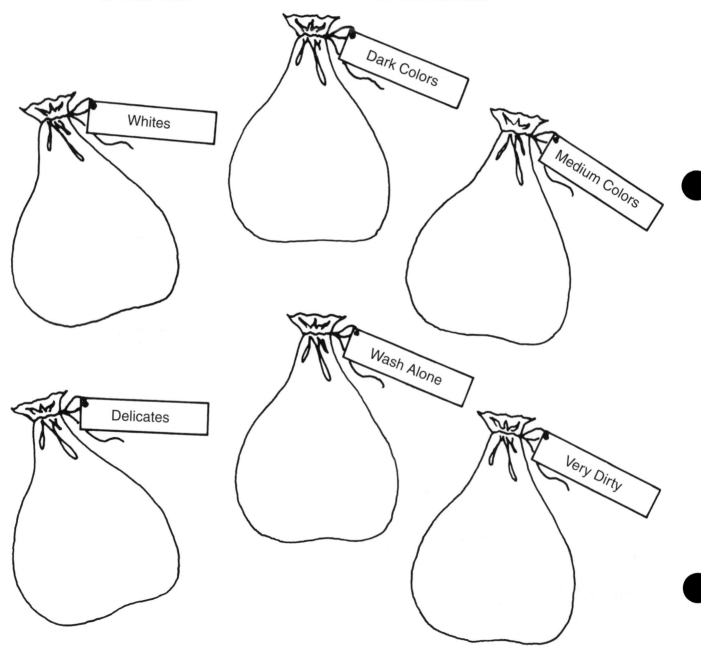

Closet Capers

Name _____

Date _____ Period _____

Place the number of the clothing item in the proper storage place in the closet.

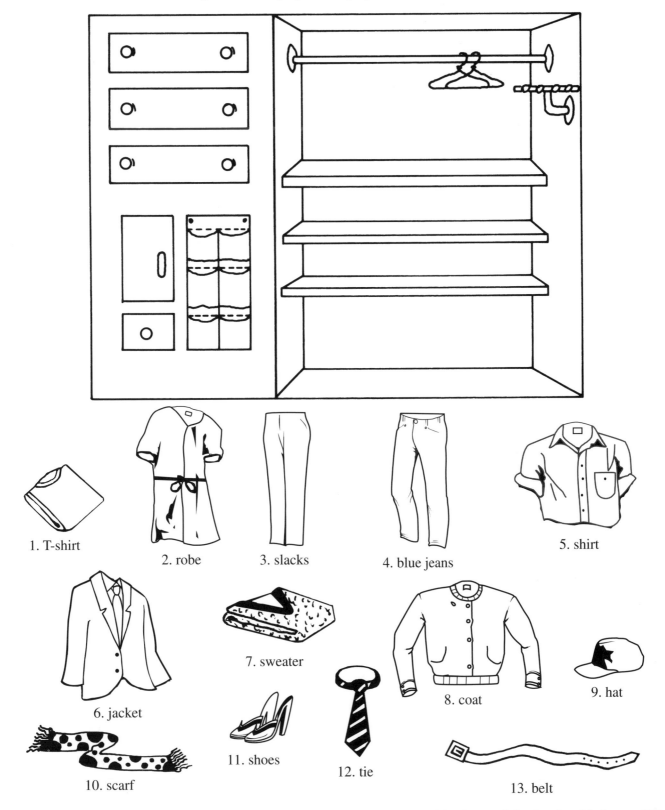

1. T-shirt

2. robe

3. slacks

4. blue jeans

5. shirt

6. jacket

7. sweater

8. coat

9. hat

10. scarf

11. shoes

12. tie

13. belt

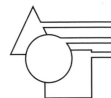

Topic 11 Learning to Sew

Sewing Machine Parts

Activity A

Name _____

Lesson 11-1

Date _____ **Period** _____

Read the use and care manual for the sewing machine you will be using in the sewing lab. Locate the following parts on your machine. Then explain the function of each part.

Part	Function
handwheel	_____
	_____
spool pin	_____
	_____
thread guides	_____
	_____
thread tension control	_____
	_____
take-up lever	_____
	_____
presser foot	_____
	_____
throat (needle) plate	_____
	_____
bobbin winder	_____
	_____
stitch length control	_____
	_____
reverse stitch control	_____
	_____

Sewing Tool ID

Name _____

Date _____ Period _____

Identify the sewing tools shown below by writing the name of the tool in the blank under each item.

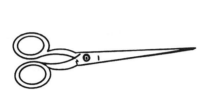

1. _____

2. _____

3. _____

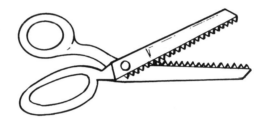

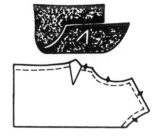

4. _____

5. _____

6. _____

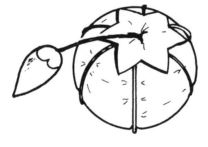

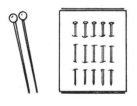

7. _____

8. _____

9. _____

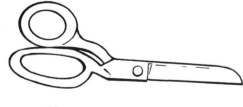

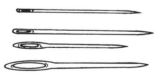

10. _____

11. _____

12. _____

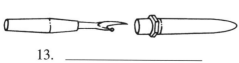

13. _____

14. _____

Tell It Like It Is

Activity C

Lesson 11-1

Name _____

Date _____ **Period** _____

The following complaints were found in the "Tell It Like It Is" box in your sewing lab. Read each complaint and write your solution to the problem.

1. Someone keeps stealing my thread! _____

   _____

   _____

2. Why can't we race the sewing machine motors? It's fun! _____

   _____

   _____

3. The people who work next to me never pick up their scraps and threads. _____

   _____

   _____

4. The class before us always takes the sewing machine needles. _____

   _____

   _____

5. My partner won't stop talking when I'm trying to sew at the sewing machine. _____

   _____

   _____

6. The teacher never comes to give me help. I never know what to do next. _____

   _____

   _____

7. I don't have anything to do while I'm waiting my turn at the sewing machine. _____

   _____

   _____

8. My partner always expects me to put the sewing tools away. _____

   _____

   _____

Where Will You Find It?

Name _____

Date _____ Period _____

You will need much information to make your sewing project. You can find this information in the pattern catalog, on the pattern envelope, on the guide sheet, or on the pattern pieces. Indicate where you will find the following information by placing the correct letter in the blank. Some types of information are found in more than one place.

A. in the pattern catalog   B. on the pattern envelope

C. on the guide sheet   D. on the pattern pieces

_____ 1. directions for sewing your project

_____ 2. the amount of fabric to buy

_____ 3. directions for cutting out your project

_____ 4. grainline arrows

_____ 5. figure type charts

_____ 6. a picture of different styles included in your pattern

_____ 7. written description of how your project will look when it is finished

_____ 8. adjustment lines

_____ 9. a list of the pattern pieces you need to use

_____ 10. the notions you need to buy to complete your project

_____ 11. the pattern size

_____ 12. directions for laying out the pattern pieces on the fabric

_____ 13. a picture of your project

_____ 14. notches

_____ 15. types of fabric suggested for your project

Pattern Symbols

Name _____

Date _____ Period _____

Below is a picture of a pattern piece. Correctly identify each symbol that has a number beside it in the space provided below. Then explain the purpose of each symbol.

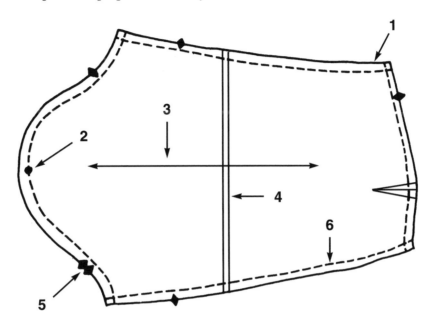

Symbol		Purpose
1. _____	:	_____
		_____
2. _____	:	_____
		_____
3. _____	:	_____
		_____
4. _____	:	_____
		_____
5. _____	:	_____
		_____
6. _____	:	_____
		_____

Sewing Skills Crossword

Activity A

Lesson 11-3

Name _____

Date _____ **Period** _____

Use the text information on sewing skills to fill in the blanks. Then complete the crossword puzzle.

Across

_____ 2. A row of permanent stitches used to hold two pieces of fabric together.

_____ 4. _____ the ends of seams to secure the stitches.

_____ 8. Fasteners used on overlapping edges that do not receive much stress.

_____ 9. A short stem that holds a button away from fabric.

_____ 10. Stitches that will remain in the fabric.

_____ 11. Always _____ seams after they are sewn to make them lie smooth and flat.

_____ 12. A method of stitching that lets you have more control over the fabric.

_____ 13. When sewing a seam, place the _____ sides of the fabric pieces together.

Down

_____ 1. When sewing on fasteners, use a _____ thread.

_____ 3. A fast and strong method of stitching.

_____ 5. Stitches that are removed from the fabric after a short time.

_____ 6. A _____ stitch is a long, loose stitch that is later removed.

_____ 7. A seam _____ keeps edges from raveling.

Fastener Samples

Activity B

Lesson 11-3

Name _____

Date _____ Period _____

Prepare two fastener samples by completing the following directions. Attach your samples to the page where indicated. Evaluate your work before turning in your samples.

Directions:

1. Cut one 10- by 5-inch rectangle of fabric.
2. Fold the fabric in half crosswise. Sew a button with a thread shank to the fabric.
3. Attach your sample below and evaluate your work.

ATTACH SAMPLE HERE

Evaluation of button: **Student**   **Teacher**

1. Stitches even   _____   _____

2. Adequate shank   _____   _____

3. Neat finishing   _____   _____

4. Button secure   _____   _____

Grade: _____

(Continued)

Name _____

Directions:
1. Cut one 10- by 5-inch rectangle of fabric.
2. Fold the fabric in half crosswise. Sew either a snap or a hook and eye to the fabric.
3. Attach your sample below and evaluate your work.

```
┌─────────────────────────────────────┐
│                                     │
│                                     │
│                                     │
│         ATTACH SAMPLE HERE          │
│                                     │
│                                     │
│                                     │
└─────────────────────────────────────┘
```

Evaluation of snap or
hook and eye: **Student**   **Teacher**

1. Stitches small   _____   _____

2. Stitches even   _____   _____

3. Stitches close together _____   _____

4. Fastener secure   _____   _____

Grade: _____

Herb Needs Help!

Name _____

Date _____ Period _____

List all the repairs and alterations that are needed on Herb's clothes. Then state what you would do to complete each repair or alteration.

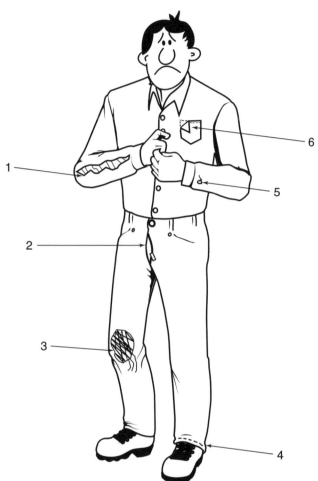

Repair needed:

1. _____

2. _____

3. _____

4. _____

5. _____

6. _____

Method of repair or alteration:

_____

_____

_____

_____

_____

_____

_____

_____

_____

_____

_____

_____

Altering a Hem

Name _____

Date _____ Period _____

Your friend has asked you to shorten one of her straight skirts. The steps you will need to follow are listed below, but they are in the wrong order. List the steps in the correct order by placing the letters in the numbered blanks.

A. Machine stitch seam tape to raw edge of hem.

B. Remove all pins and basting and press well.

C. Turn up hem on the pin line.

D. Remove old stitching from the skirt hem.

E. Pin hem in place and press the fold.

F. Measure from the fold 2½ inches all the way around and make a pin line.

G. Hand stitch the hem edge to the skirt.

H. Press out the old crease.

I. Cut the excess fabric along the pin line, removing the pins as you go.

J. Baste close to the fold and remove the pins marking the hem.

K. Put on garment and mark hem with pins using a yardstick.

L. Pin the hem edge to the skirt.

1. _____

2. _____

3. _____

4. _____

5. _____

6. _____

7. _____

8. _____

9. _____

10. _____

11. _____

12. _____

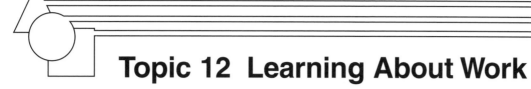

Topic 12 Learning About Work

Interview a Worker

Activity A

Lesson 12-1

Name _____

Date _____ **Period** _____

Interview someone you know about his or her job. Ask the questions below and ones that you write yourself. If possible, tape the interview and play it back for the class.

1. What is your job? _____

2. Why did you choose this job? _____

   _____

   _____

3. How does your job provide a service for the community? _____

   _____

   _____

4. What education and training did you need for this job? _____

   _____

   _____

5. What job skills are required for this job? _____

   _____

   _____

6. What fringe benefits does your job offer? _____

   _____

   _____

7. Would you recommend this job for young people today? Please explain why or why not. _____

   _____

   _____

8. What are the yearly wages for a beginning worker? _____

9. What are the yearly wages for an experienced worker? _____

10. What gives you the greatest satisfaction in this job? _____

   _____

   _____

Write additional questions you would like to ask this worker. _____

_____

_____

Effects of Work

Name _____

Date _____ Period _____

Select one of the workers listed below. Then answer the questions about the effects this person's work might have on his or her life.

farmer	florist	firefighter
flight attendant	teacher	lawyer
interstate truck driver	auto mechanic	child care director
police officer	doctor	mayor

1. Which worker did you select? _____

2. What type of income might this worker expect to earn? _____
   _____

3. How would this worker's job affect where he or she might live? _____
   _____

4. How would this worker's job affect his or her chances to make friends? _____
   _____
   _____

5. How would this worker's job affect his or her work schedule? _____
   _____
   _____

6. How might this worker's job affect his or her time away from the job? _____
   _____
   _____

7. How might this worker's job affect his or her vacation and leisure time? _____
   _____
   _____

8. How might this worker's job affect his or her sense of dignity? _____
   _____
   _____

9. What fringe benefits might this worker receive from his or her job? _____
   _____

10. How would the community benefit from this worker's job? _____
    _____

Trends and Jobs

Name _____

Date _____ **Period** _____

Select a job that interests you and answer the following questions. Indicate how the trends identified in the lesson might affect this job.

Job selected: _____

1. With more women working outside the home, will there be a greater demand for this job? _____
   _____

2. Does this job involve the care of children? _____
   _____

3. Does this job require good reading, writing, and speaking skills? _____
   _____

4. Is this a service job that involves helping people? _____
   _____

5. Does this job involve working with older people? _____
   _____

6. Can this job be performed at home? _____
   _____

7. Could this job be done using a home computer connected to an office by telephone lines? _____
   _____

8. Do you think this job could be performed by robots operating machinery? _____
   _____

9. Is this a job that involves the use of high-tech items that will require workers with technical skills? _____
   _____

10. Can a computer be used to perform this job faster? _____
    _____

Think about how you answered the questions above. Predict the future of this job. Will there be more people or fewer people in this job in the future? Explain your answer. _____

_____

_____

_____

_____

_____

_____

A Date with the Future

Name _____

Date _____ **Period** _____

Picture yourself 30 years from now. Imagine you have just been selected as "Entrepreneur of the Year." Write an article for a national business magazine about your success. Describe the early job experiences that led you to become a successful business owner. Provide any other information about your background, skills, and personality that influenced your being selected for this prestigious award. _____

_____

_____

_____

_____

_____

_____

_____

_____

_____

_____

_____

_____

_____

_____

_____

_____

_____

_____

_____

_____

_____

_____

_____

_____

_____

_____

_____

_____

Getting to Know You

Name _____

Date _____ Period _____

Complete the statements below about your interests, aptitudes, and values. Then complete the following statements about jobs that might suit you.

My best subjects in school are...	Therefore, I might do well as a...
I like to...	Therefore, I might enjoy working as a...
I am good at (list aptitudes, special talents, and skills)...	Therefore, I would do a good job as a...
I value...	Therefore, I would be happiest working as a...

Of all the jobs I listed above, the one that appeals to me most is _____

_____

because _____

_____

_____

Exploring a Career

Name _____

Date _____ **Period** _____

Select one occupation that interests you. Using either the *Dictionary of Occupational Titles* or the *Occupational Outlook Handbook,* find out more about this job.

1. Name of the occupation: _____

2. How is the job described? _____

    _____

    _____

3. What are the working conditions? _____

    _____

    _____

4. In what area of the country can this job be found? _____

5. How many people work in this type of job? _____

6. What types of companies employ people in this occupation? _____

    _____

    _____

7. What education and training are required for this job? _____

    _____

    _____

8. What specific skills are needed? _____

    _____

    _____

9. What is the future job outlook for this occupation? _____

10. What is the beginning salary? _____

11. What are some typical fringe benefits? _____

    _____

12. Why does this job appeal to you? _____

    _____

    _____

    _____

    _____

    _____

    _____

    _____

Career Goals Game

Name _____

Date _____ Period _____

Before playing the game below, list a long-term career goal on the "Finish" sign. Then decide what short-term goals must be reached to achieve this long-term goal. Write these goals on the remaining signs. Choose a partner to play the game. Use buttons, circles of paper, or coins for markers. Flip a coin to move around the board. If the coin is flipped "heads," move the marker two spaces. If the coin is flipped "tails," move the marker one space. The player who finishes first is the winner.

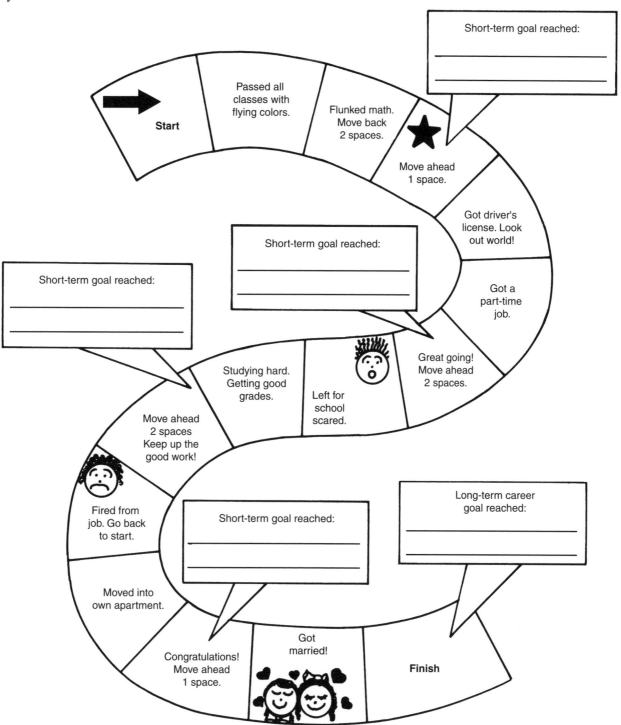

Family and Consumer Sciences Interest Survey

Activity A

Lesson 12-4

Name _____

Date _____ Period _____

Take this survey to find out which of the seven main areas of family and consumer sciences interests you most. Read each of the statements and check the answer that best describes you. Then add up your points and answer the questions on the next page.

	Strongly Agree	Agree	Disagree	Strongly Disagree
1. I enjoy cookng.				
2. I like to help people with physical disabilities.				
3. I like to help people become smart shoppers.				
4. I like children.				
5. I like to organize cabinets and closets.				
6. I like to help people solve their personal problems.				
7. I like to work on schedules and budgets.				
8. I like to tell others about family and consumer sciences.				
9. I am interested in health and the food people eat.				
10. I enjoy interior decorating.				
11. I am interested in fashion.				
12. I enjoy helping children learn.				
13. I am interested in working with 4-H and/or FHA.				
14. I like to try new and different foods.				
15. I am interested in home design.				
16. I am concerned with the way people dress.				
17. I like to manage money.				
18. I want to help homeless people.				
19. I want to design children's toys.				
20. I am exact when measuring foods.				
21. I like to sew.				
22. I like to help troubled families.				
23. I enjoy playing with children.				
24. I like working with different fabric textures and colors.				
25. I like to try new products and report results.				

(Continued)

For each *Strongly Agree* response checked, give yourself 3 points. For each *Agree* response checked, give yourself 2 points. For each *Disagree* response checked, give yourself 1 point. For each *Strongly Disagree* response checked, give yourself 0 points. Place the score you earned after the number of each question below. (Notice that some question numbers are listed under more than one category.) Then total each category. The categories with the highest scores represent the areas of greatest interest to you.

Foods and Nutrition

1 _____

9 _____

14 _____

20 _____

_____Total

Clothing and Textiles

11 _____

16 _____

21 _____

24 _____

_____Total

Child Development

4 _____

12 _____

19 _____

23 _____

_____Total

Family Relations

2 _____

6 _____

18 _____

22 _____

_____Total

Consumer Education and Money Management

3 _____

7 _____

17 _____

25 _____

_____Total

Housing

5 _____

10 _____

15 _____

24 _____

_____Total

Education and Communications

3 _____

8 _____

13 _____

25 _____

_____Total

In which area did you score the highest? _____

_____

Name three jobs in that career area. _____

_____

_____

Climbing the Career Ladder

Activity B

Lesson 12-4

Name _____

Date _____ Period _____

The rungs on the ladders below represent the three main levels of jobs for each career area in family and consumer sciences. The bottom rungs represent entry-level jobs. The middle rungs represent skilled-level jobs. The top rungs represent advanced-level jobs. A specific job is written on one rung of each ladder. Fill in the other rungs to show related jobs at the missing levels in each career area. Remember that each job should build on the knowledge and experience gained in the job before.

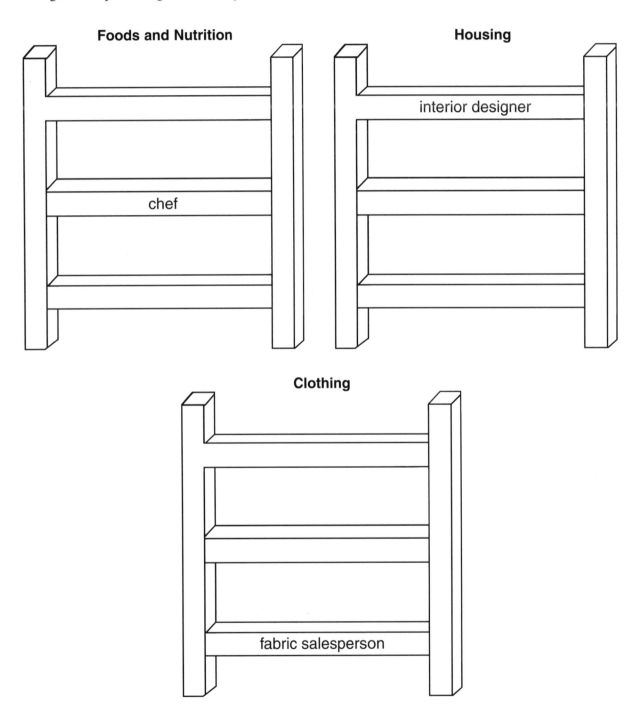

Foods and Nutrition

chef

Housing

interior designer

Clothing

fabric salesperson

(Continued)

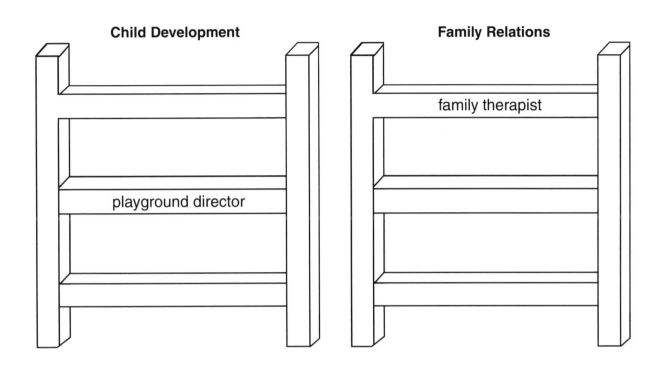

Child Development

playground director

Family Relations

family therapist

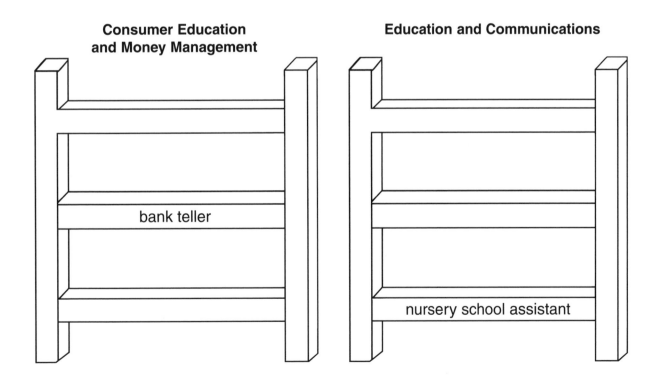

**Consumer Education
and Money Management**

bank teller

Education and Communications

nursery school assistant

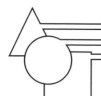

Topic 13 Preparing for Work

Planning Ahead

Activity A

Lesson 13-1

Name _____

Date _____ Period _____

Look at the illustrations below that represent different job skills. Some skills involve the use of special tools. Place a check beside each skill you already have. Place a plus sign (+) beside each skill you would like to gain. Then write a plan for gaining one of these job skills.

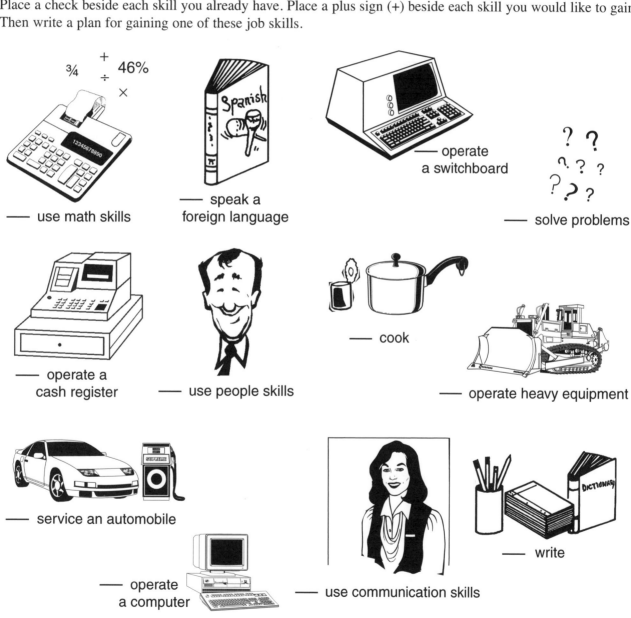

— use math skills

— speak a foreign language

— operate a switchboard

— solve problems

— operate a cash register

— use people skills

— cook

— operate heavy equipment

— service an automobile

— operate a computer

— use communication skills

— write

1. A job skill I would like to gain is _____

2. I can gain this job skill by _____

Thinking About Work

Name _____

Date _____ Period _____

Think about jobs that are available to teens in your community. List as many part-time and volunteer jobs as you can. Then list the advantages and disadvantages of working either part-time or as a volunteer.

Part-Time Jobs

1. Part-time jobs available to teens in my community: _____

_____

_____

_____

_____

_____

2. Advantages of working part-time: _____

_____

_____

_____

3. Disadvantages of working part-time: _____

_____

_____

_____

Volunteer Jobs

4. Volunteer jobs available to teens in my community: _____

_____

_____

_____

_____

_____

5. Advantages of doing volunteer work: _____

_____

_____

6. Disadvantages of doing volunteer work: _____

_____

_____

In the Future

Name _____

Date _____ **Period** _____

Pretend it is 20 years in the future. Think about the job you might have at that time. Then answer the following questions:

1. What job will you have? _____

2. What tasks will you perform on your job? _____

   _____

   _____

   _____

   _____

3. What basic learning skills will you use on your job? _____

   _____

   _____

   _____

   _____

4. What relationship skills will you use on your job? _____

   _____

   _____

   _____

   _____

5. What traits will help you be a successful worker? _____

   _____

   _____

   _____

   _____

6. What thinking skills will you use on your job? _____

   _____

   _____

   _____

   _____

7. How will you continue to grow and learn while on the job? _____

   _____

   _____

   _____

Worker's Hot Line

Name _____

Date _____ Period _____

Pretend you are the career editor for your local newspaper. In the spaces provided, write responses to the following letters readers have sent to your weekly column, "Worker's Hot Line."

1. *Dear Worker's Hot Line,*

   I made a big mistake at work the other day. Nobody knows about the mistake. I'm scared to tell my boss about it. He might fire me.

             Signed,

             Scared

   Dear Scared,

   _____

   _____

   _____

   _____

2. *Dear Worker's Hot Line,*

   I am not very popular at work. No one ever invites me to take breaks or eat lunch with them. I feel as though people are laughing and talking about me all the time. I don't like my job anyway and I'm thinking about quitting.

             Signed,

             Unpopular

   Dear Unpopular,

   _____

   _____

   _____

   _____

3. *Dear Worker's Hot Line,*

   My boss is always asking me to do tasks I don't think I can do. I'm afraid to ask her how because she might think I'm stupid.

             Signed,

             Feeling Stupid

   Dear Feeling Stupid,

   _____

   _____

   _____

   _____